I0139674

ATROPOS PRESS
new york · dresden

Conversations
and Uncertainty

By Amber Scoon

Atropos Press
(Dresden/ New York), 2017

Think Media is supported by the European Graduate School

ATROPOS PRESS
New York • Dresden

151 First Avenue # 14, New York, N.Y. 10003

Cover Design by Sarah Cassella

ISBN 978-1-940813-35-6

Acknowledgments

I wish to thank the National Endowment for the Sciences, the American Academy in Rome and Lily Library in Florence, MA.

Table of Contents

Dedication 1

Introduction 5

Santiago Zabala. Political Art 7

John Berger. Allowing Uncertainty 25

Paul Salopek. Observing Violence 33

William Kentridge. What is it To Draw? 41

John Berger. Drawing the Un-Measurable 55

Sigrid Hackenberg y Almansa. Magic 67

Margaret Grimes. Theory 75

Louise Bourgeois. Checking 87

Nick Carone. Newness 91

Paul Lindale. The Work of Art in the Age of the Anthropocene......... 99

Endnotes 107

Dedication

January 3, 2017

Dear John Berger,

This book is dedicated to you. Upon your passing, I grieve like a child. My husband told me the news. I said, "no, no, no, no!" I absolutely need you. You cannot be gone. We were going to meet in March. I wanted to introduce you to my daughter, who I know you would love. I wanted to introduce you to my husband, a mapmaker. You two would chat endlessly about making hay and drawing maps. We were supposed to drink coffee and embrace. My hero, me guiding light, my friend, my mentor, I cannot lose you.

I first read your work in 2002. I found "Selected Essays" at St. Mark's Book Store in New York City. It started a life long love of wandering through bookstores hoping to find a book that I know nothing about by an author that I do not know; a book that will change my life. "Selected Essays" traveled with me to Italy, to Portugal, to Crimea and finally to France, when I met you in Quincy. I re-read "Selected Essays" constantly. I bring it with me like a safety blanket, a source of strength. I realize, upon your passing, that all of my writing has been, in some basic way, addressed to you. And that is because you are the first artist, specifically, a drawer, who spoke to me about the process of seeing, the instinct to make art and the difference between our beautiful human desire to love, draw, see and make and the meaning that our culture, specifically our commodity

driven capitalist culture, has given to art. You were the only
one who spoke to me.

I have almost forgotten a formative experience in
my writing career. As a very young person, I wrote and I
made drawings constantly. The combination of the two
was completely natural. When I was in college, a great
separation occurred. Many of my studio arts professors
actively discouraged me from writing, thinking, questioning and involving myself with philosophy. One of my
professors asked in disgust, "Are you a painter or are you
a philosopher? You have to decide." A college friend, who
made a great impression on me, was the child of New
York intellectuals: writers. In their company, I was a naïve,
unsophisticated, small town kid. And though my artistic
talent was recognized, it was clear that I could not be a
writer. Writing was reserved for a certain kind of person,
with a certain kind of intelligence. Writing was reserved for
someone who had the correct vocabulary, who understood
politics and could be witty and quick minded. I was none
of those things and I was embarrassed about my impulse to
write. For the most part, I kept quiet.

Sometime after I finished my master's degree in painting, I wrote a twenty-page essay about my experiences. It
was partly a travel story. It was partly a philosophical essay.
It was partly poetry. It was partly a reflection on the process
of making. My parents, with good intentions, encouraged
me to share the essay with a professional writer who they
happened to know. He read the essay and told me that it
could not be published. He said that I needed to decide if I
wanted to write a novel or non-fiction, about travelling or
about art, a personal story or an objective essay. In short, I
had not respected any genre of writing and the result was
that my writing was un-readable.

Upon meeting you in Quincy, in 2009, I decided that I could write. I told you my fears and you encouraged me and gave me strength. I wrote *Quantum Art*. My greatest achievement is that you read *Quantum Art,* and you called me to tell me that you enjoyed it and learned from it. You said, "Go on!"

This book, *Conversations and Uncertainty*, was born because of the conversation that I had with you, that summer in your house in Quincy. Speaking with you was a beautiful event. It was storytelling. It was a philosophical exploration. It was a drawing in the making. I felt the sensual and intellectual joy of being present in the world, of observing the world, of sharing the world and of loving the world, simultaneously.

In the moments after I realized that you passed, I suddenly felt that I could no longer write. I had thought that writing was like drawing, a thing that I would do automatically and intuitively, regardless of whether or not anyone noticed. But I was wrong. I was writing for you. I am comforted only by the idea that you held dear, the idea that the dead are still with us. After your mother's death, you met her in Lisboa. You spoke to her. You saw her. You learned from her. I will look for you in Napoli. And I will continue to write to you.

Conversations and Uncertainty is dedicated to you.

Sincerely,
Amber

Introduction

Santiago Zabala suggests that there is a difference between a dialogue and a conversation.[1] In a dialogue, the outcome has been predetermined. In this case, it's more like a performance, with language and content that have already been set. Everyone knows what to say and how to behave. In a conversation, you don't know where the ideas may go.

John Berger speaks to his dead mother in *"here is where we meet."* He writes, "I risk to write nonsense these days. (His Mother replies) You put something down and you don't immediately know what it is. It has always been like that, she says. All you have to know is whether you're lying or whether you're trying to tell the truth, you can't afford to make a mistake about that distinction any longer."[2]

In these essays, I try to allow for possibility at the risk of ending up with nonsense. I observe these conversations and interactions, along with the thoughts, images, memories, drawings and objects that surround them. Sometimes, I observe a moment as brief as a scent that surprises me and disappears before I can recognize it. Sometimes, I observe conversations that are continuous and interwoven into my daily life. In each case, my observations are based on lived moments. They are without proof, record or measure. They gather into a steady, strong swell and then recede into an imperceptible hum. They mimic each other, each time returning slightly altered. In writing these essays, I want to give them space.

It is my hope that when you read these chapters, you will also allow for the space of uncertainty, possibility and the unknown. Certainty is demanded of us, in our every day life, with such relentless vigor that we respond continuously with packages of certainty. In reading, writing, thinking and making art, we have a choice. We can allow ourselves to bask in the deliriously disorienting and gorgeous confusion of this mysterious world.

Santiago Zabala

Political Art

I. To Make Art is Political

Santiago shocked my students with this simple idea: To make art is political.[3] Let me re-phrase that. The activity of art making is, in and of itself, political. It is political because it is a conscious decision to do something *else*. It is a choice to do something that does not automatically fulfill the pre-determined demands of the framework that we live within.

The act of making art is a small rebellion. It is the child who says, "I will not do my homework. I will climb a tree and listen to the crows." We know that in order to survive in the world, the child must learn to do his homework, regardless. We tell her so. We say, "Do your homework!" But we are secretly pleased when she finds a way to escape.

John Berger writes, "I still have a dream in which I am my present age with grown-up children and newspaper editors on the telephone, and which nevertheless I have to leave and pass nine months of the year in the school to which I was sent as a boy. As an adult, I think of these months as an early form of exile, but it never occurs to me in the dream to refuse to go."[4] Making art is an attempt to refuse exile.

But is the activity of art making in and of itself a political activity? Are there some types of art that are political and some that are not? Is there an ethical imperative to make political artwork? And if so, what does it mean to make political art?

II. Charlie Hebdo

The contemporary art world is uncomfortable when political art gets too close to propaganda or illustration or consequences. Of course the line between art, propaganda, illustration and consequences is nebulous. And that liminal space is so generous. Liminal, coming from the latin, means "threshold". It is the piece of wood on the floor of a doorway. When standing on a threshold, we always have at least three opportunities: stay where you are, come inside or go outside.

Charlie Hebdo, the French satirical magazine, famously became the center of a terrorist attack because of a cartoon drawing of the prophet Muhammed. In the art world, it is inconceivable that a drawing could cause 12 deaths.[5] Unthinkable.

What makes a drawing a cartoon? And what is the difference between a Charlie Hebdo cartoon and political art?

Prior to the 19th century, a cartoon referred to a preparatory drawing: a map for an artwork. It would eventually be covered by a painting or fresco. In the 19th century and onward, a cartoon refers to a drawing that creates satire or humor. They must be realistic enough to communicate a clear message and they are generally published with text. A cartoon has clarity, language and widespread distribution.

Although the Art World sympathizes with Charlie Hebdo in this particular case, it does not consider Charlie Hebdo's cartoons art.

III. Guernica

Picasso's Guernica is almost universally celebrated as one of the greatest anti-war paintings in history. It's an enormous black, white and grey painting depicting the moment of agony in which women, children and animals at a market place in Guernica, Spain, were bombed. It was Monday, April 26, 1937. The bombing of Guernica is considered one of the first instances of an aerial attack on defenseless civilians. Women and children were deliberately targeted.

Although Franco's regime was officially neutral during World War II, Franco was ideologically aligned with Hitler, Mussolini and Facism. It seems that the bombing of Guernica was carried out with the help of Hitler and Mussolini's forces.

Guernica, spelled *Gernika* in Eskara language, is considered the spiritual center of Basque Nation.[6] The Basque region is an antonymous region, isolated from Spain by geographical barriers and separated by language and an independent culture. Franco was having trouble taking the Basque Nation. The bombing was a symbolic attack, designed to break spirits rather than destroy cities, soldiers or artillery.

At the time of Guernica's exhibition, Picasso was criticized for *not being political enough*. The painting was commissioned for the 1937 World's Fair in Paris. It opened on May 25, 1937, just a month after the bombing of Guernica. It drew attention to the event. But that attention must have seemed ineffectual in relation to the brutal shock of death.

In 2008, I stood before Guernica in the Reina Sofia Museum in Madrid.

Picasso did not sell Guernica to his dealer as he did with his other paintings. Instead, the painting toured Europe until the victory of Franco in 1939, at which point the painting was sent to the United States for safe keeping. It was used to raise funds for refugees escaping Franco's Spain. Exile, Refugees, Pain, Resistance. It continues today.

In 1939, Guernica was exhibited at the Museum of Modern Art in New York City as part of a retrospective for Picasso. The exhibition opened just weeks after the Nazi invasion of Poland.

In Picasso's will, he requested that Guernica be returned to Spain when the citizen of Spain again enjoyed "public liberties and democratic institutions". After Franco's death in 1975, Guernica was returned to Madrid, Spain.

I stood before the painting, at the back of the room, behind a hoard of other viewers. I started to draw. Drawing is a way to be honest about looking. You need time. Seeing is layered. It has moods. It has moments of ecstasy and moments of discomfort, moments of gorgeous humming clarity and moments of confusion. Seeing a painting is like listening to an album. It's different every time you hear it, every time you imagine it and every time you taste it.

My sketchbook rested on my left hand. My right hand was drawing. I was standing flush to the wall, without touching it. I began to get tired. I leaned back so that I could rest my shoulders against the wall. The guards immediately told me to step away. I complied. Still later, exhausted, I tried to sit, crossed legged, on the floor. The guards immediately yelled. No Sitting! The crowd turned to look at me. I scowled. The guard looked shocked and disgusted. I was not even allowed to be mad. I was supposed to stand still, murmur quietly and move along.

A friend once told me, "Do not sit on the ground of a piazza in Italy." I was trying to make a long drawing and I couldn't stand for the entire time. I asked, " Why?" The piazza was safe. The stones were warm. And it was comfortable to sit at the edge of the piazza. He replied. "Only peasants sit on the ground, only *la schifezza e i poveri.*" Only the dirty and the poor sit on the ground.

IV. A Call to Action

Philosopher Marshall McLuhan's suggested that "The medium is the message" in his 1964 text "Understanding Media: The Extension of Man."[7] The nature or context of the medium is itself, the content of the artwork.

Artist Filippo Minelli painted the words "Flickr," "Facebook" and "Youtube" on the walls of buildings in slums.[8] The mark-making tool, paint, is standard. But the support, the walls of slums, changes the meaning of the image. This artwork instantly becomes political, not because of the content of social-media but because it calls our attention to an impoverished population that does not enjoy the same access to technology as the wealthy.

Minelli's artwork is not exhibited on the walls of slums. The photographs of the walls of slums are exhibited in galleries. Santiago writes, "The Italian artist's photographs are not points of arrival for our aesthetic contemplation but rather points of departure to change the world."[9]

A call to action is, in and of itself, political. Right?

V. The Problem

Let's examine the problem.

The world that we live within, become within, make art within is unjust. This is clear. What should we do? One response to injustice is political action. But can we believe in political action in a world in which democracy is relentlessly corrupted by capital? And how does a visual artist respond to a situation of injustice with a language-less medium?

William Kentridge discusses Plato's "Allegory of the Cave." Kentridge writes, "The man who has seen the light

and apprehended the understanding that follows from
it has a duty to return to the cave, to unshackle those in
darkness, and to bring them up from the cave into the
light. If necessary, this must be done with force. The nexus
of enlightenment, emancipation, and violence emerges.
Our agenda has been set."[10]

Plato creates the ethical demand: seek out the truth
in an unjust world and help your fellow humans escape im-
prisonment. Inaction is inexcusable.

Alain Badiou makes it clear that our contemporary
situation is one of global violence and unacceptable injustice. He says, "Liberal capitalism is not at all the Good of
humanity. Quite the contrary; it is the vehicle of savage,
destructive nihilism."[11] If I participate in such a system,
am I not condoning it? In a post-World War II mentality,
silence is unacceptable. Silence is compliance.

Should Heidegger's philosophy be refuted because of
his affiliation with the Nazi party in 1933?[12] And in the
future, will contemporary artists be dismissed because they
made art within the system of global capitalism? Will future artists not be asking, "Why didn't they *do* anything?"

On September 11, 2001 I was at Ground Zero, working with the Salvation Army. We were delivering coffee,
food, and clean socks to firefighters and recovery workers.
I later learned that a friend of mine was also there, a friend
that I was worried about. But she was not there as a recovery worker. She was there on her own, to take photographs.
I cried. When I heard this news, I was sitting on a stoop
outside of Bellevue Hospital. I was there to provide food
and water to people waiting in line. They were lined up to
identify the remains of bodies at the morgue. I could not
see the end of the line.

The situation of global capitalism is not equivalent to Nazism. However, similar questions arise. At what point is political inaction inexcusable? At what point is artwork, as a response, not *enough*? How can a person effect change, without violence, when the system is corrupt? How can we effect change when the system uses political dissent to its benefit in order to pacify the very people it disserves?

We are told to appreciate democratic capitalism because we have the theoretical possibility to live secure, healthy, peaceful lives. But why should we accept such a bleak reality? Most of the Western world lives in fear and ill health. Badiou writes, "Evil is decisive. Under the pretext of not accepting Evil, we end up making believe that we have, if not the Good, at least the best possible state of affairs—even if this best is not so great. The refrain of "human rights" is nothing other than the ideology of modern liberal capitalism: We won't massacre you, we won't torture you in caves, so keep quiet and worship the golden calf."[13]

The question is, is there a possibility for something *else*? Can we create a more just and healthy world? Can we escape the Anthropocene?[14] And what is the role of art in all of that?

VI. Alain Badiou

Badiou writes, "An event is the creation of a new possibility. An event changes not only the real, but also the possible. An event is at the level not of simple possibility, but at the level of possibility of possibility."[15]

I want to create an event that allows for the possibility that art has infinite undetermined possibilities.

In 2010, I attended Badiou's class in Saas-Fee Switzerland. I had travelled overnight from Boston to Geneva via

London. Upon landing, I took a train to Visp. In Visp, I
took a bus to Saas-Fee. The morning I arrived, I walked up
the hill and found Badiou's class. I was high in the Alps,
inside the clouds. The only way to get higher was to take
the gondola that disappeared further into the clouds. I
took that gondola once, with a Palestinian-Lebanese *Jesus*,
who informed us that he had been in several plane crashes,
with a shy intelligent boy from Chicago who seemed to
have anxiety about nearly everything and with Gregg, who
has a fear of things moving without his volition. And me.
I'm claustrophobic. We had a collective panic attack. We
walked down.

    This was my third summer in Saas-Fee. I came specif-
ically to study with Badiou. I sat in the back of a packed
classroom. Badiou has the kind of magnetism that draws
warm, expectant, dense silence. He has the elegance of a
movie star, although his speech is interrupted by coughs.
At the end of his lecture, he told us, "I am a very old man
and this may be my last trip to the mountain." He thanked
us for what we had given him - our silence, our questions
and our curiosity were a gift to him. He is a giant: generous, humble, poetic, intelligent and beautiful.

    As I sat through three days of Badiou's lectures, I was
slowly becoming more and more ill. Dizzy, I listened as he
provided a history of the connections between mathematics
and philosophy. On a piece of paper, I wrote my question:
'What is the place of quantum physics in the relationship
between math and philosophy?' It was the first question
that he read and he was upset that I had not put my name
with the question. He demanded, "Who wrote this question?" I couldn't speak. He was upset. He did not wish the
question and answer period to be anonymous.

He answered. "In classical physics truth equals determination. In classical physics truth can be calculated in anticipation and in reflection. Truth can be verified. In quantum mechanics, truth involves both "the event" and "chance" (Badiou's exact words). The event is a rupture in the expected repetition of life. And chance is the possibility for something to happen in that rupture that could not be predicted with accuracy. Quantum mechanics gives us the idea that events cannot be predetermined with certainty."[16]

When we think of art as an Event, we accept that we cannot predict its outcome. We cannot direct its meaning. How then can we use it as a tool for social and political change?

On the fourth or fifth day that I was in Saas-Fee, I found myself in the backseat of a car, with two crazy East Germans, racing down hairpin turns, trying to get to the hospital in the city of Visp. The great philosopher Theodor Adorno was born on September 11th, 1903. The East Germans joked that I was in good company. Adorno too was rushed to the emergency room in Visp, and he died there in 1969. On the way back up the hill, one of the East Germans lost his stomach. To both of them, I am eternally grateful.

VII. Jorge Luis Borges

"Then the revelation occurred. Marino saw the rose, as Adam had seen it in Paradise, and he realized that it lay within its own eternity, not within his words, and that we might speak about the rose, allude to it, but never truly express it, and that the tall haughty volumes that made a golden dimness in the corner of his room were not (as his vanity had dreamed them) a mirror of the world, but just another thing added to the world's contents. Marino achieved this epiphany on the eve of his death, and Homer and Dante may have achieved it as well."[17] This is part of a short story called "The Yellow Rose" by Jorge Luis Borges.

The rose and the artwork are related to each other,

each other.

Deeply ingrained in our minds, there is an assumption that our reality is singular. And this absolute faith in a finite reality creates the possibility for a second: a copy. But there is no original. There are only endless possibilities. It follows that copies are not seconds, but new events. The act of mimesis is a creative activity, which allows an event to become itself.

VIII. John Berger

John Berger writes, "And the naming of the intolerable is itself the hope."[18] Is it our ethical responsibility to point out the intolerable? Politics, it seems, needs language, and if not language, than clarity, and if not clarity, than metaphor. A metaphor points toward language and clarity.

But how can we name the intolerable without naming tools, specifically, words? If art exists in a nameless, language-less state, how can it become political?

John Berger writes in the introduction to *Collected Essays*, that the social and political activity of art is the ability to provide a comparison between one point of view and another. And the difference, the difference between what *you* see and what *I* see, provides "an increase in awareness of different potentialities in different people."[19] It creates a space where people allow themselves, each other and their environments, more possibilities.

An increased awareness of the differences between how people see and sense the world expands possibility. This activity has little to due with the subject or content of the artwork. An increased awareness is the result of the process of observation. It matters less *what* you observe and more that you become aware of the activity of observation.

By paying attention to sensations of observation the artist is widening her awareness of the uncertain and the infinite. There is an acceptance for repetition (I observe myself drawing every day) and an allowance for rupture (I am unsure of what I will find as I draw today).

But does an increased awareness of potential and possibility equate to political art?

IV. Walter Benjamin

Walter Benjamin wrote that art making would necessarily become political with the advent of technological reproduction (the film camera, for example). When an artwork can be reproduced easily, it looses its "aura": the authenticity of uniqueness that is associated with a one of a kind object. He writes, "But as soon as the criterion of authenticity ceases to be applied to artistic production, the whole social function of art is revolutionized. Instead of being founded on ritual, it is based on a different practice: politics."[20] Also, "for the first time in world history, technological reproducibility emancipates the work of art from its parasitic subservience to ritual."[21]

But repetition fails to make art political. Why?

Capitalism is an animal that eats endlessly until it dies of obesity. Art does not escape this situation. Repetition doesn't make art political because repetition doesn't change capitalism. On the contrary, capitalism feeds off from it.

With the advent of technological reproduction, artwork
did not become "the object designed to be reproduced."[22]
Artwork became the object designed to be sold.

It is naive to think that selling one's artwork is an
activity that occurs *after* the art-making process. At best,
it affects the art-making process. At worst, it guides the
art-making process. Regardless, if the artwork exists inside
the framework of contemporary art, one of its functions
is to create profit. Profit is often disguised by ideas like
education, activism, culture, philanthropy, charity, therapy
or the love of art.

Technological reproduction fails to destroy our deep
reverence for the original. We like to believe that art's mar-
ketability is simply proof of its importance; its position as a
true original. An original object is something that"belongs
to or pertains to the origin," something that is "not a copy
or imitation." The origin doesn't need to pertain to the
physical or singular object. The origin exists in our minds
as an idea.

Technological reproduction and postmodernism gave
us the idea that art's originality can pertain to the artist's
idea, method, material, workshop, leadership, context,
mark, attitude, school, rules or myth. The origin can be his
PR campaign, his Facebook presence or his imagined identity. The aura of the origin exists regardless of how many
times we copy.

X. Plato
Plato tells us in *The Republic* that desire must be set aside
in order to prioritize the needs of the greater good.[23]

What is the true desire of the artist?

Do artists desire progress, activism, political and social rights, international peace and so on? Or are artists' desires poisonous and destructive like Schopenhauer's unrelenting and torturous will? Must we set aside our desires in order to access art and truth? Is political art an attempt to direct the artist's natural desires toward a respectable and ethical outcome?

XI. Jean Luc Nancy

The activity of philosophy is the activity of creating choice where before there was certainty.

Jean Luc Nancy points out that although many artists today claim that their work is political, we in fact, do not even know what this word 'political' means. Nancy shows us that there are many facets to the word 'politic.' It can refer to a philosophical idea of the city. It can refer to politicians. It can refer to laws, nations and power relations. It can refer to personal beliefs.

The origin of the word 'political' comes from the Greek word "*Polis.*" It means "the coming together of a community." So what part of the word '*political*' are artists striving for when they claim to produce socio-political artworks?

The community who views contemporary political artwork is often not the community that the artwork attempts to address.

How are the people living in slums affected by Filippo Minelli's artworks? If you live in a slum and you do not have access to the Internet, how do you feel about having the word "Facebook" written on your walls?

XII. Napoli, Italy

In Napoli, Italy, sometime in the late 90s or early 2000s, I was tear-gassed by police. At first I thought it was just me. I rubbed my eyes. My lungs burned a bit. I was confused, but not alarmed. Then, I realized that the whole crowd, a packed football stadium, was uncomfortable. And then panic set in: a collective desire to move, to run. And it was at that point that I became aware that the hoard of people inside the arena wanted to escape, all at once, as if we were one body. In numbers like that, with limited exits, we were unable. If Vesuvio erupts again, it will be difficult for all of the citizens of Napoli and the surrounding area to leave fast enough to survive. It is the densest city in all of Europe. And there are simply not enough ways out. "Vedi Napoli e Poi Mouri." That's what they say, "See Naples and You can Die."

What happened after the tear gas happened quickly, like fire running along a gas spill. We could not orient ourselves. Suddenly there were police in riot gear everywhere and mazeltov cocktails and windows breaking and buses on fire. You are tumbled by a wave and you swim hard toward the surface, determined and calm. You prepare to break through the surface, but instead you touch sand. Fear. This was about soccer, but also about poverty, drugs, trash and the mafia.

The fertile landscape outside of the city of Napoli has become the dumping ground for Europe's toxic chemicals.[24] Companies pay to have their toxic waste shipped south and disappeared. After decades of toxic dumping, animals have mutated and no longer reproduce. Women miscarry. And people die from what locals simply call, "The Illness."

Journalist Roberto Saviano went under cover in order
to document the activities of organized crime in South-
ern Italy. He published his finding in his book *Gamorra*.
The Camorra, the organized crime group whose capital is
Napoli, issued a death threat against Saviano. He lives in
Napoli still, but with a permanent police presence.

The text, *Gamorra*, became a film under the same
title. Matteo Garone, the film producer, has not been
threatened. Despite the film's popularity, it seems that the
Camorra is completely disinterested in the film, *Gamorra*.
What is the difference? The text was taken as journalism, as
truth. The film on the other hand was taken as art, as imitation. The film (the artwork) was assumed to be harmless.

In 2010 the artist Filippo Minelli was diagnosed with
Non-Hodgkin Lymphoma and was not expected to live.
He did live and he made an artwork about the experience.
The artwork included dirt from the soil that he played in
as a child. The soil was contaminated by PCB's.[25] There is a
clear connection between PCBs, toxins and illness. No one
tried to kill Minelli for making a political artwork. Instead,
the phenomenon itself tried to kill Minelli. And what is
the phenomenon? A complex situation involving companies,
governments, policies and customers, in which, in the name
of profit, toxins are created and dumped, despite the fact
that toxins kill. Who is held accountable for this injustice?

XIII. Plato's Demand

Plato demands that art defend itself. What better way to do
this than to create an artwork whose activity and function
is social awareness and political betterment?

XIV. Questions

What if, when we think about art, we do not answer art's pre-determined questions: "How can you prove that it is original, new and transcendent? Does it contribute to new knowledge and truth? How will it change our world?"

What if we ask different questions? What if we ask no questions?

What would it be like if every time we had sex, we faced each other and asked, "How can we prove that this activity is worthwhile? Did it teach us something new about ourselves? Did it make us healthier and wiser? Did it add to our collection of knowledge? Did it help us transcend or current state of affairs? Did it help us connect to each other, ourselves and our world?'

It's not that a couple *can't* answer these questions. They can. It's just that these questions are not necessarily related to the instinct to have sex. And further, asking these questions doesn't make sex better.

It is difficult to think about art without asking our pre-determined questions. It is difficult to know what questions to ask, if any. But I believe that it is necessary to strip art of these questions and then ask, "What are we left with?"

Artists are not dumb, blind, voiceless creatures that create by divine intuition and random luck. But that myth is there for an important reason. It exists because of the need to acknowledge the gap between the rational, Newtonian, Enlightenment thinking that guides our contemporary, everyday lives and *the way that we experience being in the world.* There is a beautiful, liminal space between the desire to make art and the way that art is understood, taught, experienced and explained.

XV. The Being of Art Comes Before

The being of art, the instinct to make art, the desire, the force that drives us to keep making art despite the fact that no one believes in it, that it is a terrible career choice for everyone who is not living on a trust fund and that our culture demands that we do anything and everything *except* make art - that *being*, the *being* of art, comes before. It comes before language. It comes before culture. It comes before economics. It comes before truth. It comes before seeing. It comes before ethics. It comes before politics.

What we do with it, once it is made, is assign meaning. And the meaning that we give to art has more to do with our beliefs than the instinct to make art.

XVII. If We Let Go

If we let go of our beliefs about art, what happens?

I am not only the twenty-one year old who ran all the way from the West Side Highway to the 14th Street Salvation Army Center and got in the back of a truck with a girl who told me, "I saw them jump." I am not only the girl who delivered coffee to firefighters who told me about finding the body parts of their buddies, who proposed to me on one knee. I am also the terrorist who flew those planes. I am also the three year old who saw the Lebanese War of 1982. I am also the dead whose bodies I stepped over. I am also the mother. I am also the son whose father was killed by the mafia when he couldn't afford the protection fees and his storefront was bombed. I'm the child who survived the bombing and whose mother re-married the chief of police. I am the chief of police who taught the boy to deliver forged documents and sleep with a pistol beneath his pillow. I'm the one who lays awake wondering if and when a girlfriend can be taken for ransom.

If it does not matter if you made it or I made it, if you
did it or I did it, if I am to blame or you are to blame, if I
hurt you or you hurt me, if you died or I died, how would
it change the way that we make art? If our desires were free
to roam without names or origins, what would we make?
If our desires were free to roam, without fear of evaluation,
retaliation, poverty and shame, what would we make? If
our desires were free from fear, what would we make?

How could this letting-go change our understanding
of political art? I suspect that what we might make would
not be recognized as art.

John Berger
(November 5, 1926–January 2, 2017)

Allowing Uncertainty

I met with John Berger the summer after my second
semester at the European Graduate School in Saas-Fee,
Switzerland. I had written to him. I wrote a rather long
letter, explaining who I was and why I was so interested in
his writing. To this day I regard him as the most important
thinker about art. Maybe it is because he is also an artist,
the kind of artist that actually likes to draw. I probably told
him more than I needed to in my letter. I agonized over it.
Should I give him the painful details, the personal details,
the dramatic ones? Should I keep it short and intellectual?
I did not keep the letter. It was too embarrassing to care so
much about a person that I didn't know. And too painful
to show a complete stranger how much I care about art and
people and survival and fear. I asked him if I could come
visit him. He sent me a hand written note. He said that I
should come visit him and that we would make hay. I
was stunned.

My visit was long. We sat outside. We ate an egg and
ham dish at a long rectangular table in the yard behind his
house. A nearby baker made the dish and John told us her
story. We drank wine and talked.

It is difficult to decide what to tell you about this
visit. I was very impressed by the way that he ignored flies.
Have you ever tried to ignore a fly as it sits on your food,
on your nose, on your fork? John Berger ignored them so
well that I wondered if he even saw them. But then, he

must have. He was sprightly. He moved with the enthusiasm of a kid. He was incredibly sharp and awake. I want to be that present. I think that drawing can help us to be present. Also sleep and good health. I was impressed that he had an outhouse. And as I write this, I think, 'Can that be right?' I was impressed that he lived in a rural place. Isn't it hard to do these days? We gravitate to cities where you can no longer smell the dirt, the sunset, the rain. John still helps with the work of the farm. I got lost, trying to find his home. I asked a neighbor if the writer, John Berger lived nearby. The neighbor replied that he did not know of any writer, but that there was a man with a motorcycle. His grand daughter danced around the table and gifted us with flowers. You could tell that these flowers were quite magical. All of these things made sense.

I wrote down three ideas of his, which I meant to share with you. But now, they do not seem as important as the fact that if we had had the correct weather, we would have been talking while making hay. Our bodies are important. And John Berger can ignore flies that sit on his face, his hands, his fork and his food, as if they absolutely do not exist. As if he had disappeared them with the power of his mind.

I am reading, in preparation for writing this essay, *here is where we meet*, by John Berger. In this book, he recounts a story about visiting the grave of Borges with his daughter.[26] He recounted this story to me when I visited him. Is it a story that he has told many times?

I have also told the story of visiting John Berger many times, always to my students with regards to the three observations. Each time that I re-tell the story I doubt myself. Am I remembering it all correctly? I'm sure that I accidentally change small details each time that I tell the story. Or maybe the pure act of remembering is changing the past, just as my imagining is surely changing the future. And I wonder if John Berger remembers that day and if, when he remembers that day, he changes me?

Here are the three things. He told me, "Do a job for money that allows you to do research for your art. It may not be a job that is recognized by the art world as an art job." This struck me as extremely good advice, and advice that almost no one would take. I am an art professor. It is the most obvious job to have. Does it serve as research for my art? Has it become a resource of visual and sensual information? Does it provide me with chances, accidents and interruptions? My father used to tell me, 'Relationships can give you energy or take it away. You have to decide.' When you are in a relationship that is not very good, you really need to think about this question and it feels difficult to answer. When you are in a good relationship, and for me this has only happened once, it is very simple to answer. It is difficult to say whether my job gives me more than it takes. I believe that academia is one of the worst places for art to thrive. My colleague, Louis Katz tells me, 'Who is the biggest patron of the arts today? Academia. Academia is your patron'. I am immediately worried about this. When the church was the largest patron of the arts, the subject matter of paintings was biblical. Can we honestly say that every artist desired to make biblical paintings? I think artists condemned their desires before they ever emerged. I don't want to make the art that my patron condones. Worse I don't want to make art for my patron, thinking that it is the product of my own desire.

The second big idea that I remember is this: Make your art community out of people that you care about as opposed to people who you believe should care about art.

In other words, give equal value, if not more, to the activity of sharing art with those people who you love. That seems quite simple, but it rarely happens. One problem is that in America it's difficult to create any community, period. So you come to rely on people that are pre-designated to care about what you care about. You invite art people to your art opening and call it a day.

I've shared this idea with so many academics: Let's make our art community out of the people that we care about and the people that we find interesting, regardless of whether or not they are part of the art world. Nearly all of them had this reaction: "But non-artists do not understand art. We need those who are educated in art in order to decide what is good. We need some system for evaluation". In other words, if your artwork is not shared with academics, curators or pre-determined art viewers, you will never know if your art is worthwhile. But more accurately, you are simply not an artist at all. It is the validity of evaluation that makes the contemporary artist an artist.

I do not believe that it is important *for artists* to assign value to their art. I believe it is helpful (although not necessary) for artists to share their work with others. But this is a distinctly different activity than asking, 'Is my work good?' If the artist is being herself, the work she made is necessary. It makes no difference if it is good. It had to be made. Evaluating artwork that is necessary is like evaluating the sexual acts of two people who are in love and desire each other. It doesn't matter if it is quick or messy or graceful or awkward. It makes no sense to ask. It could make sense to ask the audience, if there were in audience. In that case, the sexual activity becomes pornography or performance. Regardless, the question 'Is it good?' is for the *viewer*.

Art and love, I believe, are the only activities of radical and true freedom. Art is to academia what love is to porn. You can learn something about sex while engaging in pornography or learn something about art making while in school, but it would be a mistake to credit this kind of learning with the ability to make art or love. We must be careful to provide space for art and love outside of their given uses and functions even if it means that we feel partially invisible.

One problem with the capitalist, academic, viewer-critic is that he is not really an expert. The designated viewer, the one who decides if art is good or not, is simply not in a position to decide. Why? Because he is not practicing the activity he evaluates. If there were to be evaluators, they should be other artists. That is almost never the case. Regardless, critics (artists or not) cannot discuss art's value without incorporating its market value: a fabrication based on investment strategies and academic bureaucracy. This evaluation is meaningless.

The value of art and the value of art evaluators are both null. This contemporary state is actually wonderful. When we strip objects, activities and environments of their predetermined meanings, including their accepted functions and characteristics, we allow them a space to change. This is the beauty and openness of nihilism. This chance for change is needed. We need it for survival. We need it for art. We need it for play. We need it for health. We need it for pleasure.

Artists don't need to know if their art is good. The importance placed on external evaluation, is not a reflection of an artist's needs. It's a reflection of our culture's needs. Most artists cannot retain their natural inclination to allow the being of art to exist. They obliterate their natural inclinations by adhering to the demands of their times: global capitalism, the scientific method, the need for newness, communication and originality, and lastly the absolute need to be validated by a pre-determined external source. The artist is buried under the heavy image of the artist.

John Berger looked at my art. As is the case with very few artists, there was no discussion about what he liked or what was good. He told me that he believed that I needed to paint water, but not ocean water and not lake water. He thought that I needed to paint clear moving water, stream water. I should observe water, through which, many layers reveal themselves: water currents, colors, rocks, sand, reflections and sunlight. This was his third piece of advice.

When I arrived back to Syracuse University in upstate New York, I had an experience that became routine. I shared the story of my visit with my students. My enthusiasm was met with dismay. These students could not stand the thought of art theory, of aesthetic philosophy, of the problems of contemporary art, of *talking about art at all*. They acted like hurt teenagers. To them, all I was saying was 'You can't just make things and expect financial success'.

So what is the problem here? Why are young people so burdened by ideas when artists, historically have been both makers and thinkers? Why has thinking become the enemy? Why has talking about art become a prescriptive, judgmental, no-end disaster in the minds of so many young artists? Why did my dear colleague, Jim Jeffers, tell me that when he first read 'Ways of Seeing' by John Berger, he was incredibly discouraged?

This discouragement is so important. We can't discard it like a stoic adult dismisses a child's tantrum. This is a moment of pain. We have to pay attention. What is this pain? It is the great 'Accident of Art' that Paul Virilio speaks about.[27] It is the unmentionable. It is the fact that no one knows what art is, but people still believe in it. We, as contemporary artists are in a moment of immense and unspeakable vulnerability. It is especially felt by young artists. Vulnerability turns to anger when it is not cared for with the empathy of a mother for a sick child.

Where I see openness, my students see fear and insecurity. Contemporary American culture breeds a need for security, clarity and certainty. It creates an illusion that these things exist. My students expect clear problems, methods of problem solving and evaluation procedures. They demand well-defined careers and the promise of success, which is exclusively defined by money. They desire the financial security needed to survive as well as the financial delirium that accompanies the idea of fame.

My students view the Accident of Art as an annoyance and a problem that needs to be solved. I see the Accident of Art as an incredible opportunity for imagination, creation and open-ness. I love the fact that we do not understand the nature of art, just as we will never understand completely the nature of love. I am happy that art doesn't easily fit the model of market capitalism or politics or activism or communication. What it means to be an artist, today, in 2017, is a mystery. I want to embrace the excruciating vulnerability that comes with not knowing. I want to allow the vulnerability of art to exist.

Paul Salopek

Observing Violence

I.

When I was young, I remembered stories from when I
was very old, which was before I was born. I stood at
the pumps at the Sunoco Station where my dad worked,
telling the mechanics these stories while we waited for the
ice cream truck. There was nothing shocking about these
stories. I grew up playing in the woods. The woods were
safe and things died and went into the ground. From the
ground things grew. Death was all around us in the woods
and it was intimately connected to birth. This felt normal.
I should mention that I grew up without religion and that
I did not understand that people believed in God.

Paul Salopek is walking around the world. He is
following the path of human migration. He estimates that
it will take seven years. His project is called "The Out of
Eden Walk".

John Berger writes, in *here is where we meet*, about
speaking with his dead mother in Lisbon. She tells him
that in the beginning there is always a death and that
this death starts the desire. The desire is the desire to fix
something, to change something, to make something just a
small bit better.

When I was small I noticed the smell of things rotting,
vultures picking at dead animals, trees struck by lightning,
a frost killing the crocuses in March. I never felt that there
was something wrong that needed fixing.

II.

A drawing, it seems, doesn't really start until you begin to fix it. You get it all laid out, making a mark for all the important points that you see, just so that you can go back in and start to fix it. It's going to be wrong at first. Necessarily. The exciting part is erasing, moving, re-drawing, erasing again, watching the world around you resist your attempts, watching your drawing disappear and re-appear, watching it breath.

When you draw what you see, in your outward world and your inner world, then, with each mark, with each lifting of your eyes, your world will emerge and change. Your drawing, then, will change. And you are happy because you desperately want to be *a part* of the world.

III.

Paul is walking out of Africa. The images that he brings back are largely of suffering, of displacement, of war, of unspeakable human evil. He told me, when I met him at Princeton University, that when he arrives to a new city, he imagines what it would look like if it were bombed out.

What happens to our minds and bodies when we consistently witness violence? What happens to the cells of the body, to our matter, to the water, to the bones, to the connective tissues, to our organs, to our neuro-passageways?

Each time that we observe something, we enact mimesis. We observe it. We recognize it. We name it. We connect ourselves to it. We try to place it in a context. We remember it. We dream about it. Sometimes we write about it, draw it and photograph it. And we think of it each time that we see a new city.

What do we do, when a violent reality surrounds us? I am not asking about ethics. I am simply asking, "What is happening when we observe violence?" This may be the single most important question that an artist can ask.

We can try to allow for kindness and family and peace in the hopes that it will combat images of terror and pain. In this case, it's a battle of the will. The images of violence will arise without warning and the self responds by inviting an image of non-violence. In some cases of PTSD, the mind erases horrific memories. But even when we cannot recall the images, the pain remains: a phantom limb that aches in cold weather even after it has been amputated. Our body produces the pain of the process of mimesis even without the conscious ability to remember, to think, to feel. We sense fear without holding any image in mind. This is a pure form of panic.

IV.

I believe, in my heart, that art comes from a place of complete safety. William Kentridge said, "Art arrives from a place of safe uncertainty"[28]. This is the kind of infinite possibility that only very small children feel, if they are blessed with a moment or two, in which they cannot imagine violence, terror, illness or pain.

V.

When we observe violence, we replay it in our minds. Do our cells also replay it, repeat it, recall it and re-create it? Can the mimesis of violence make us sick?

If we see nothing but war, is it physically possible, to imagine something peaceful and safe? Can we suspend our belief if our beliefs are entrenched in fear? Is there a point in which there is no room to imagine or recall playfulness, calmness and joy?

Sontag writes that those who experience war can never explain it to those who have not. She explains, "We don't get it. We truly can't imagine what it was like. We can't imagine how dreadful, how terrifying war is; and how normal it becomes. Can't understand, can't imagine. That's what every soldier, and every journalist and aid worker and independent observer who has put in time under fire, and had the luck to elude the death that struck down others nearby, stubbornly feels. And they are right."[29] There is no window from which we can safely view the other side.

So why do we try to tell each other about war and poverty? Do we somehow believe that copying it, if only on paper or film or words, will help to *fix* this world? Or do we copy our worlds because that is how we survive? Do we copy our worlds because it is an instinct; an instinct that some can quiet and others cannot?

Once violence has become normal, can we be surrounded by a normal that does not include violence? Or does it drive us crazy, to see violence, as we repeat it in our minds and bodies, while our daily reality goes on without violence? Isn't it better, if your normal includes the constant image of violence, to be somewhere where every other body and every other set of eyes sees it too? Isn't it better not to be alone?

Maybe, the process of *mimesis*, of copying and observing our worlds is, in part, the activity of trying not to be alone. Our bodies, from the moment of conception, are engrossed in the relentless process of duplicating. Alan Lightman writes, "In fact, most of our body cells are constantly being sloughed off, rebuilt, and replaced to postpone the inevitable. As one might imagine, the inner surface of the gut comes into contact with a lot of nasty stuff that damages tissue. To stay healthy, the cells that line this organ are constantly being renewed. Cells just below the intestine's surface divide every twelve to sixteen hours, and the whole intestine is refurbished every few days."[30]

Christians break bread to symbolize the body of Christ and drink wine to symbolized the blood of Christ. We want to eat his body and drink his blood.[31] To eat him, to hold him, to merge his cells with yours, was, or still is, to add his greatness to yours. Have we really come so far? Can *mimesis* itself, simply be the process of gathering more?

A possible definition of *mimesis*: to gather as much of the world as possible into one's arms at once.

VI.

Our bodies have the ability, both to observe and to observe our selves observing. The ability to observe our selves is a fundamental characteristic of consciousness. We create a self to watch the first self. In this way, mimesis and consciousness are intimately related. And our senses, our mimesis technologies and our consciousness are greatly affected by our speed of observation.

From a plane, we observe the world differently than from a car. From a horse we observe the world differently than on foot. From a run, we observe the world differently than from the steady pace of a walk. From behind a camera, we observe the world differently than from a naked eye. As Heisenberg writes, "We have to remember that what we observe is not nature itself, but nature exposed to our method of questioning."[32]

Marina Abramovic's recent performance, "*The Artist is Present,*" illuminates the power of looking. Abramovic sits in the Museum of Modern Art in New York City. One by one she invites a member of the audience to sit across from her. She lifts her eyes to meet the other person's gaze.[33] No one speaks. No words are exchanged. Over and over, the performance made people cry, overcome with the emotion of making a present and simultaneous connection. Two people look at each other. Two people observe each other. Two people create each other. Two people re-create each other. Slowness.

VII.

I believe that we want to feel our own matter become entwined with the world around us. We want to be in love: with the world, with each other. We want to re-connect ourselves to the dead: to the rotting trees, to the old people that we once were, to all those that we have lost, some before we were even born. Is it possible that we are more aware of this process at certain speeds?

If the only way to connect with each other and with the world, is through the touch of violence, than the desire for connection will overcome any desire for peace. And if you have never seen peace, you may not desire it at all, because desire is a function of mimesis.

Mimesis comes first.

In a timeless, simultaneous, quantum state, we could mimic the images of the past as well as images of the future. We could have access to peace and play at the same time as horror and poverty.

Maybe it is the separateness that is the thing that is broken. The separateness is the thing that we want to fix. We want to feel what we know to be true, that we are the world around us, inseparable, without the passing of time, in the ever-present moment, intangible like stream water. We want to feel that death is intimately connected to birth, that one does not happen before the other, but that both are happening at the same time, at once, always and now. We want to hold it all; to become the world.

I was once completely open to the uncertainty of the world. I regarded it without judgment because I had no need to protect myself. You have to be safe to allow for that kind of uncertainty: infinite possibility. There was no need for the term magic, because everything was already possible. I could learn how to fly and speak to trees.

I can't see the world like that now. I can't suspend my beliefs. Partly because I have too many. The bigger problem though, is that I cannot allow myself to suspend my beliefs. To be totally uncertain now is too dangerous. I am afraid that part of that mysterious world is evil. So I try to maintain control over my understanding of reality. It's a tragedy.

I do have the capacity to not believe, somewhere within me. And every day I will search for it.

William Kentridge

What is it To Draw?

I.

David Brett wrote, in an essay about John Berger and
Marisa Camino's drawings, "What is it, to think? What is
it, to draw? It must mean, to have uncertainty."[34]

Drawing is a space and a moment, in which things are
nameless and curious, as we were, in a time before we can
remember. It is a return to our selves; a return to a space
without fear of dissimilar things whose relationship is
unclear. There's you and me, for example. There's no need
to fear that you are seeping into me and I am seeping into
you. It's already happened.

Alain Badiou writes "every work of art is a description
without place."[35] We could also say that a work of art is an object or space that has been detached from its environment and
that it is the activity of mimesis that enacts its detachment.

Badiou suggests, "It is that sort of movable reciprocity
between existence and nonexistence that constitutes the
very essence of drawing. The question of drawing is very
different from the question of Hamlet. It is not 'to be or
not to be,' it is 'to be and not to be'. And that is the reason
for the fundamental fragility of drawing: not a clear alter-
native, to be or not to be, but an obscure and paradoxical
conjunction, to be and not to be."[36]

Drawing is a process of collecting all of the possibilities
that exists at once, even if they appear to contradict each
other. Is the tree alive or dead? It is both.

Drawing appears to be fundamental to the human being; an instinctual process. It is something that all children

41

do naturally, with or without instruction. It is something that most adults abandon. And so, it is important to ask: What are we doing when we draw?

The history of drawing predates language and reminds us that the un-namable exists. We looked at things and drew them, before we could speak their names. Rather than attempt to translate drawings, we might attempt to experience them with the same discomfort and joy that accompanies and drives the activity of looking. Drawing reminds us that the world is more mysterious than we assume it is. It sits before us, constantly and incessantly. It beckons us to face it with humility. As we draw, we situate ourselves in relation to this world. And as we draw, we fail. Or rather, we cannot situate ourselves once and be done with it. The world keeps changing and knocking us out of our place. And so we try again and again. Maybe this is what the human activity of drawing really is: an attempt to connect ourselves to the unnamable world.

We encounter the unnamable world in our own bodies. How incredibly strange to be housed in a body that operates according to rules that we cannot know. What is that pain in my shoulder? What is that sensation in my torso? I don't know. I can't ask. Even if I tear it open and look at it, I still don't know. Even if I take photographs of my brain, I still cannot know. Who is in charge in there? And why don't I have direct access to my cells, my neurons, my organs, my very own immune system?

Drawing is one way in which we observe our world. What is the nature of this observation? It is unclear. I ask "What is it To Draw?" in order to call attention to the uncertainty and potentiality of drawing. We have yet to take it into consideration. I sense that the instinct to draw is the instinct to close the gap between looking and being: to become the body instead of trying to look at it: to become the world instead of observing it, to loose, in some way, the self-awareness that makes us feel the distance between our selves and our worlds.

II.

I first met William Kentridge at the American Academy in Rome. My late professor Terry Kirk had arranged a studio visit. Kentridge wasn't happy to see us, but also wasn't unwelcoming. We looked at each other without speaking, a silent acknowledgment. The American Academy in Rome was incredibly clean, quiet, spacious and civilized, so far from my life in Napoli, which was packed tightly with colors and shapes; unpredictable, colorful, dirty and loud.

We had interrupted Kentridge at work. First, I noticed charcoal. Then, my eyes rested on the paper, large enough to let the whole arm swing, lit by the beautiful light coming into the studio through his window. Last, I saw his hands, large and dirty with charcoal. I do not remember his body.

In Sevastopol, during the Orange Revolution, I suffered from intense stomach pain. My friends told me to eat charcoal. I couldn't imagine eating the material that I had used so often in figure drawing classes, the material that Kentridge used to make his art works. Eat the charcoal? I did it.

In Kentridge's studio, the charcoal had been moved and erased so many times that a pile of erased charcoal left a fluffy, velvet line on the floor. I imagined gathering all that charcoal in my hands. It would be warm and greasy, with pockets of air and pockets of grime. And it would feel good like lake mud on a warm summer day.

The paper showed evidence of a long journey: hours
and days and the ache of a hand. Trying to understand
the paper was like stepping into a room in the middle of a
story, a story so complex and packed with characters that
you can never hope to orient your self. Instead, you settle
for the sound of the voice and the energy in the room. I
felt the richness of the charcoal, the intensity of the black,
the deep space created in the erased areas, the movement
of the marks, quick and agile, the endless searching and
fixing, erasing and re-drawing. It was clear that moving and
erasing occurred, not because the drawing was wrong, but
because it was alive and all living things move.

Kentridge didn't disguise the charcoal. The inconsistencies of his hand were there. The wear on the paper
was there. The energy and fatigue of his body were there.
He was making a single drawing in charcoal. Every few
moments he took a picture. Then he would erase a portion,
re-draw it, change it and take another picture. Later all of
the photographs were strung together, like a flipbook. In this
way he was making films from animated charcoal drawings.

III.

I've seen Kentridge's charcoal drawings before they became
animations. And I've seen them as films, animated and
projected. What is the difference between the two?

What is the change that takes place when we subject
our drawings and images to certain processes of mimesis?
What changes when our drawings become prints, photographs, cast objects, films and projections? Benjamin
wrote, in *The Work of Art in the Age of Mechanical Reproduction* about the political and philosophical transfor-
mations that accompany the activity of making multiples.

But what is the aesthetic transformation, the sensual one, the purely physical change? I am convinced that the reason that humans are drawn to images made through mechanical and digital processes of mimesis is precisely because these processes remove the hand. When we remove the hand, we create the illusion of consistency. We eliminate or mitigate the constant inconsistency of our own bodies.

Regardless of their place in the history of technology (printmaking is relatively old where photography is relatively new), the processes that interest me here, are the processes by which drawings become something *else*.

When a drawing becomes a print, a plate with the image of the drawing, is rolled through a printing press. The printing press provides constant, steady, equal pressure. This makes the mark consistent in a way that the hand never achieves. When you remove the question of numbers (making one drawing versus one hundred drawings), you are left with this difference: the press removes the hand, if only by a few degrees, whereas the drawing keeps the hand, completely.

The inconsistency of the hand becomes especially clear when we add speed. The longer and faster we work, the more inconsistent our hand becomes.

We are fascinated with processes that show us what we are not: consistent. We look at paintings that appear to be made without a hand, so perfect, so utterly removed from the imperfections of our own bodies and we say, 'Do you see the brush marks? No! Is it a photograph or a painting? Incredible!' The obsession with the removal of the hand is larger than we think.

Drawing is an activity that keeps the hand. It can't help it. It doesn't keep the hand for the sake of political resistance or philosophical inclinations. It keeps that hand because that's what drawing is: a mark made with the body: a documentation of the drawer's existence in her world.

IV.

At the time that I met Kentridge at the American Academy in Rome, I was doing something akin to his process in my studio. I was using oil paint and found materials to make a painting. Then I took a slide of it. Then I worked on it again. I changed it. Sometimes I wrapped it like a present. Sometimes I dug into it like an archaeologist. I took another slide. By the time I was finished I had 20 slides and the painting weighed so much that I had trouble carrying it.

I showed the slides with a slide projector on a concrete wall in my grad school studio, which was the basement of a parking garage in a neighborhood of Rome known for prostitution. We walked past needles and abandoned cars on our way from the bus stop to our studio. Later, my professor, Terry Kirk committed suicide and was found in his car somewhere near the studio. At least that is what I was told. I could never bear to look closer at the details.

The slides were pretty. But I didn't care about them. I cared about the layered object that I had made, which was now a heavy solid block completely covered in hardened glue and wrapped with fibers. It didn't look like anything special. I managed to get it home in a suitcase that weighed too much and I never wanted to exhibit the painting.

The project, as an artwork, was a failure. The images, the slides, had lost something. And the object, the painting, lost its layers to its unreachable insides. It didn't work. I had to move on. My colleagues were upset that I would throw out something that looked good. But why should I apologize or regret? You can't regret waking up or needing to pee. I'm not making the things to create good-looking objects that people will like. If that were the case, I would paint landscape paintings of the most beautiful places on earth. In fact, I would love to do that. But there is something in my way. And it isn't a choice. It's a necessity.

V.

What is the instinct that drives us to make art?

We cannot define love by saying that it is a function of procreation. Love exists with or without procreation, before it and after it. There are many possible functions for activities like love, art and thinking. But those functions do not tell us the nature, essence or identity of these activities. The functions of these activities only tell us about the values of our society. In our case, art's function is commodity: monetary commodity, intellectual commodity, educational commodity or cultural commodity. The best we can do in this circumstance is to try to negate the commodity by considering the artwork a gift or by enacting disbelief.

Regardless of a culture's appointed functions for artwork, thinking and love, we continue. We make art. We think. And we fall in love. It appears that we just can't help it. Will there be a time when we no longer fall in love, no longer sit lost in thought and no longer watch children run towards the water in order to make marks in the sand? I don't think so. I believe that these things are more fundamental than our ability to use language or make tools.

As a child, I made many time capsules. I wrote about my experience in the woods. I wrote about the events that took place, the creatures, their families, the trees and their intricate, complicated lives. I translated the languages of crows and rocks. I collected special stones and leaves. I spent time sitting in particular places that were designated meeting places, where I would be given the important news from the woods. I buried the time capsules. And although I drew maps of where they were, I was never concerned about digging them up. To this day, there are many in the ground.

VI.

Many years later I showed Kentridge's charcoal animations to students. I found myself telling them about what the paper looked like before it was photographed. I told them that it was an overcast spring day in Rome, spreading warm, even light on a very large piece of paper. It was large enough to let the whole arm swing around. I tell them about the velvety nature of the charcoal and the line of charcoal dust on the floor. I tell them that the erasure marks were alive and energetic and exciting.

VII.

The second time that I saw Kentridge's work in person was at the Metropolitan Opera at the Kennedy Center in New York City. I was there to see *The Nose*. It was the fall of 2013, almost a decade later. I was pregnant at the time: nauseous, nervous and excited. I got up to head toward the bathroom because I was going to throw up. The workers who stood at the door told me that if I left the interior of the opera house, even just to use the bathroom, I would not be allowed back into the Opera. So I turned to walk back to my seat. And as I walked, I threw up on the floor. We were on the balcony level, where the cheapest tickets were. I laughed.

The Nose made me feel like a kid. I couldn't understand what I was seeing. I couldn't understand the words, which weren't in English anyway. I couldn't read the subtitles and see the opera at the same time. I couldn't name the elements of the performance and I couldn't describe the whole. There were drawings that became sculptures that became architecture that became people. There were figures that I thought were drawings but later began to move. There were figures that I thought were humans who became drawings. There were doors that I thought were images of projected light. And from the projected doors, real humans walked out into thin air.

The Nose is an opera, inspired by a musical arrangement, inspired by a book, written by a Russian writer, who was provoked by the endless frustration of human incompetence and absurdity. And it was all funny even though I couldn't understand a thing! A man lost his nose. And that big nose was running around on its own, causing a ruckus. For all of its strangeness, and its complicated history, the opera felt contemporary and normal, as if, of course a man would spend his days searching for his mischievous nose.

XIII.

I can't draw the human body. I used to, but it's been at least a decade that I cannot.

In 2002, I made portraits, from observation, of the people who lived and worked on my block in Flatbush, Brooklyn. It was a special time, post 9/11 in New York City. I was alienated from my class and my professors at NYU. I was at home in my neighborhood. One of my professors had said, on the morning of 9/11, before I went to volunteer with the Salvation Army, "Isn't it beautiful?" One of them had said, when I returned to class, months later, at a late night critique, "Amber is like Joan of Arc. She went to Ground Zero to volunteer. But the rest of us? We feel nothing." I cannot forgive them.

My senior thesis exhibition took place in Manhattan. I stood there watching professors who didn't know me, examine the work. The department head said, "These paintings are excellent. Why don't I know this student? " I remember thinking, "Because you're an ass." I didn't even know him. I was angry. I exhibited the same paintings at my local library on Cortelyou Road in Brooklyn. The people that I had painted, mostly shopkeepers from an immigrant neighborhood, far removed from the art world, came to see the paintings. They came to see themselves. I was happy, like a child is when she makes a present for her parents.

Since then, I have tried many times to draw humans. I start and then I stop. I think about it, I plan it, I get excited about it, but then, I find myself, in the studio, doing other things. I make an intention to draw the body and then I abandon it. It is not a matter of ability or discipline, but something much more crucial and difficult. It is something like pain, but when I try to inspect it, I am overcome with fatigue. Against my will, I begin to daydream.

In a small class with Paul Virilio, in La Rochelle, France, Virilio introduced himself by shaking each of our hands, one by one. It was a hello by the touch of two hands. He didn't shake, actually. He took each hand into his and held it for a moment. He did the same with our eyes. Later, during his lecture, he said that the history of artwork in the twentieth century is the history of artists mutilating the body. Artists abstracted the figure. They cut it up and re-arranged it. They distorted it, destroyed it and violated it. Virilio said that the history of the twentieth century was a history of incredible violence done to human bodies. And so, the artist's reaction would have to be the same: to create images of bodies only to destroy them.[37]

How can we observe bodies without destroying them, mutilating them, violating them? If the bodies we see are dead, what are we doing when we observe them?

X.

In Kentridge's version of *The Nose*, he managed to confuse me so thoroughly that I was lost in a pure sensory experience.

Why was I so struck by Kentridge's charcoal drawings, the ones that I saw that spring day at the American Academy in Rome? I think the charcoal alarmed me because I felt Kentridge's hand. It was so intimate, even though he was a stranger to me. I felt the sensation of his seeing, the speed of his making, the inconsistency of his hand, and the presence of his body. I was embarrassed and fascinated.

Everything about his hand was unlike me. I couldn't pretend to belong. I tried to become the objective, intellectual art viewer that art school had taught me to become. But instead I found myself inside the drawing and the hand of Kentridge, which had become one with the drawing. Although I knew that I wasn't invited into that space, I couldn't bring myself to leave. It was like trying to wake myself from a dream which keeps pulling me back into it.

It seemed to me that Kentridge was observing his dreams, his life, his body, his imagination, his ancestors' memories, his many possible futures, all at once, with the same energy and ability. It was all real. It was undeniable and real.

Kentridge made me question: "Can you imagine past what you know? Can you imagine past what you believe?"

XI.

Some years later, in the Spring of 2016, my students and I witnessed a strange thing. The walls that rise above the Tevere, the river that runs through Rome, were being cleaned. Workers scaled the walls with ropes and scaffolding and pressure washed them. As the walls were being cleaned, images beneath were revealed. Layers of grime were removed. Underneath the grime, there were old bits of graffiti that wouldn't budge. They were ghosts of images. They were bits and pieces. It felt as if an archaeological dig was being conducted, which slowly revealed an ancient layer of drawings.

For several days, we watched the dark grimy wall get cleaned.

One evening, I saw a horse. I was crossing the Ponte Vecchio, a foot bridge that connects Campo di Fiore to Trastevere. The fragments of darks and lights that remained on the wall suddenly connected themselves. At that very sharp moment, the entire wall, many times taller than me and so long that I could not see it all at once, became one huge drawing. A moment earlier, I saw some dirty bits of a wall, some clean bits of a wall and some echoes of ancient graffiti. Then suddenly, I saw Kentridge's horse. It was a horse that I had seen many times in *The Nose*. I was stunned.

I left before the drawing was complete. Kentridge was making a giant eraser drawing, using a pressure washer to remove the dark organic matter that grew naturally on the wall. The dark matter that was left became animals and humans and vehicles, all walking in a slow procession. And it was their arrival, their appearance, unannounced and unexpected, arising from nowhere, that seemed so magical. Before the images appeared, their possibility did not exist in my mind. The wall was a quiet thing that called my attention only because of the workers who pressure washed it. I saw them, for the first time, from above. I stood on tiptoe, leaned over the wall and looked down. And I thought, "If I fall from here, I will die." I looked to see that the workers were well connected, that they would not fall.

And now, that quiet wall had become a space, an event, a procession, a horse! Suddenly it was real. Suddenly it existed whereas before it had not! I could feel the presence of both at once. I was grateful for that moment. It was a gift.

John Berger
(November 5, 1926–January 2, 2017)

Drawing the Un-measurable

During the summer of 2015, John Berger and I spoke about drawing the un-measurable.

What is un-measurable? It is some thing or some place, for which boundaries and reference points cannot be precisely located or determined. The un-measurable may disappear or change its form or location at the instant that measurement is attempted. The movement occurs at the *very same moment* of measurement, as if the act of measuring and the subject of measurement were intimate strangers, entangled in a simultaneous dance, connected by mysterious forces.

The un-measurable has been connected to ideas of God, magic, mathematics and the infinite. In latin, "fin" indicates "end" and "in" means "not". The infinite is therefore something without end, something without borders. It is thought to be an abstract idea; something we can think about but not experience.

In quantum physics, the term "indeterminancy" indicates that by its own nature, a quantum system does not have a unique set of measurable properties and values. A quantum system denies our fundamental beliefs about measurement, namely that objects can be measured if the correct measurement tools are available.

Can we observe without measuring? Can we draw the un-measurable? What happens when the un-measurable observes us?

In response to these questions, John Berger and I wrote the following texts, drew the following drawings and shared them via post.

One or two pages about vigilance

A good many people have their favourite bars where they like to meet friends and share a drink. I prefer drinking with friends at home. But I do have my favourite municipal swimming pools, where I go to swim up and down at my own pace, crossing other swimmers whom I don't know, although we exchange glances and sometimes smiles.

Such pools have nothing in common with the private swimming pools of the well-off, or with the luxury pools of the very rich, who today are catastrophically buying up the future of the very planet on which we live.

The wearing of bathing caps is obligatory. As is also a shower with shampoo before diving or stepping down a corner ladder into the pool. I dive and as I swim my first strokes under water I have the sensation of having entered another time-scale, somewhat similar to the feeling a child may have at home when he decides to go from one floor to another.

As swimmers we share a kind of egalitarian anonyminity. No shoes, no marks of rank, just our swimming costumes. If you accidentally touch another swimmer whilst passing him or her, you offer an apology. The limitless cruelty towards others like ourselves, the cruelty of which we are capable when we are regimented and indoctrinated, is difficult to imagine here as you turn to swim your twentieth length.

The outside walls and the flat roof of the municipal pool are of glass. So from the water you can see the surrounding buildings and the sky. To the west there is a slope of grass at the top of which grows a large, tall silver-maple tree. I watch this tree as I swim on my side.

The overall form of the tree with its many upward thrusting branches is like the shape of any one of its leaves. (This is more or less evident for most varieties of tree.) The maple leaf is pinnate shaped- reminiscent of a feather. (The Latin for feather is pinna.) The face of the leaf is a salad green, its back is a greenish silver. The inscribed destiny of the maple is to be pinnate.

I decide to make a drawing of it as soon as I get out of the pool : a sketch of the whole tree and on the same page a close-up drawing of one of its leaves. Like this, I say to myself, still swimming, it will refer in some way to the maple's genetic code. It'll be a kind of text of a silver maple tree.

Such texts belongs to a wordless language which we have been reading since early childhood, but which I cannot name.

(drawing)
(text of silver maple)

58 Conversations and Uncertainty

Later I swim on my back and look up at the sky through the framed glass roof. A vivid
blue with white cirrus clouds at an altitude, I'd guess, of about 5000 m. (The Latin for curl is
cirrus.) The curls slowly shift, join, separate as the clouds drift in the wind. I can measure
their drift thanks to the roof frame ; otherwise it would be hard to notice it.

The movement of the curls apparently comes from inside the body of each cloud, not
from an applied pressure ; you think of the movements of a sleeping body.

This is probably why I stop swimming, and put my hands behind my head and float.
My big toes just break through the surface. The water below holds me.

The longer I gaze at the curls the more they make me think of wordless stories. wordless stories like the stories fingers may tell, but in fact here stories told by minuscule ice crystals in the silence of the blue.

drawing
(text of air currents)

Yesterday I read in the Press that twenty Palestinians in their homes were blown to pieces in Gaza, that the U.S.A has covertly dispatched 300 more troops to Iraq to defend their interest in the oil refineries, that James Foley, an American journalist held as hostage by the Isils was filmed during the ritual of his execution by beheading, and that 35 illegal immigrants from India, men, women and children, were found suffocating in a shipping-container on a freighter that had just crossed the North Sea to dock in London.

The cirrus is drifting northwards towards the deep end of the pool. Afloat on my back, motionless. I watch it and chart with my eyes the pattern of its undulations.

Then the assurance the sight offers changes. It takes me time to understand how. Slowly the change becomes evident and the assurance I receive becomes deeper. The curls of the white cirrus are observing a man afloat on his back with his hands behind his head. I'm no longer observing them, they are observing me.

Check tomorrow details of the street protest march against the new World Order next week …

September 10, 2015
Corpus Christi, Texas

Dear John,

I made this drawing while looking out the window of a plane. I often draw while flying.

On the first day of classes at the European Graduate School, Wolfgang Schirmacher asked the students to describe our current cultural situation in one word. I said, "Panic." That June, in 2008, in Saas-Fee, Switzerland, so high up in the Alps, we spent three weeks inside the clouds. Since I arrived in the clouds, I had no idea what my surroundings looked like. It was like arriving in the night and waiting three weeks for daylight. It was also the summer that Air France Flight 447 mysteriously crashed into the Atlantic Ocean. In 2012, it was finally announced that the crash was due to temporary inconsistencies between airspeed measurements.

There are a group of people who are planning to go to Mars, even though it seems clear that there will be unable to return to Earth: a total untethering. These are competitive, intelligent, passionate people. They all have a choice.

As a child, I once felt myself drift above my body, floating about five feet above myself. I'm told that this is called dissociation: the state of being disconnected or separated from something else. In this case, I was becoming disconnected from myself. Maybe I was not disconnecting, but doubling?

As an adult, I had a dream like this: I was floating. I was about as high as you are about twenty minutes before landing in a plane, just as you exit the clouds and see nearly every detail of the ground below. I was looking down onto a house without a roof. The kitchen was small and square, with a rectangle table in the middle. There were no people. To the left of the kitchen, there was a very small bathroom, with only a toilet and sink. To the right of the kitchen, there was a bedroom, slightly smaller than the kitchen. At the corner farthest from the kitchen, there was a single bed and a child's wooden dresser. There was a little girl in the bed. I cried in my dream as I have never in my waking life, with nothing but sorrow. The child, who was me, had died. I think of going to Mars as another way to watch your own death. I can remember the dream as if it were happening now. The pain does not soften.

As a child, my husband climbed the stairs of a house that his parents built in Fredericksburg, Texas, into a loft, where he could lay on his back and watch the clouds through a skylight. The skylight acted as a viewfinder, creating particular compositions by isolating one small portion of the sky.

The changing compositions inside a skylight are a constant surprise. It's mesmerizing like watching a fire, but more soothing. It is the delicious delight of both calm and wonder, oneness and connection.

James Turrell has a permanent installation at PS1 in New York City called "Meeting House." It's a room with a hole cut out of the ceiling, with wooden chairs that allow you to recline and view the sky. It was one of the first artworks that I saw when I moved to New York City. Turrell shows us nature itself: clouds, sky and the occasional plane. What is more amazing than nature itself? Art is always poor, in comparison.

In the spring of 2016, I looked up at the hole in the ceiling of the Pantheon in Rome. I thought about the roundness of the building, the roundness of the hole and the peace that I felt. It didn't occur to me that above the hole, there was sky. I saw that grey-blue hole as a flat plane, as if a painted canvas hovered over the hole. Then, suddenly, clouds raced by. At once, I became aware of a very deep space. The Pantheon, which until then encompassed me and held me in space, became a very small circle, floating in a vast, incomprehensible and infinite world. I felt a brief sensation of floating. The clouds changed the light. The circle in the ceiling, which I had thought was perfectly symmetrical, revealed itself. It was full of imperfections and inconsistencies.

I look outside of the plane. There are beautiful, luscious, enormous, fluffy clouds, just below me. They change shape and move too quickly for me to draw. I look. I make a mark. I look again. I have lost my place. I try several times, without success. And then, instead, I begin to draw the shadows that the clouds make on the ground. The shadows stay put longer. The land is absolutely flat with only slight variations in green and brown and the shadows of the clouds are a warm blue-purple-grey. They look like wool blankets, resting on top of the land. I make a quick drawing.

As I drew, I realized that the clouds look solid. They have the texture and pattern of sand on the beach, where the sand meets the waves, when the waves recede back towards the sea. After looking and drawing for ten minutes, I *only* see the clouds as a plane of solid ground. I imagine running my hand over the surface of the clouds the way you can run your fingers over a metal washboard, creating a pleasing thud, thud, thud, thud. It was only my belief that nagged the washboard sand back into becoming clouds. When I stopped drawing, I realized that my clouds resemble a flock of birds.

With Love,
Amber

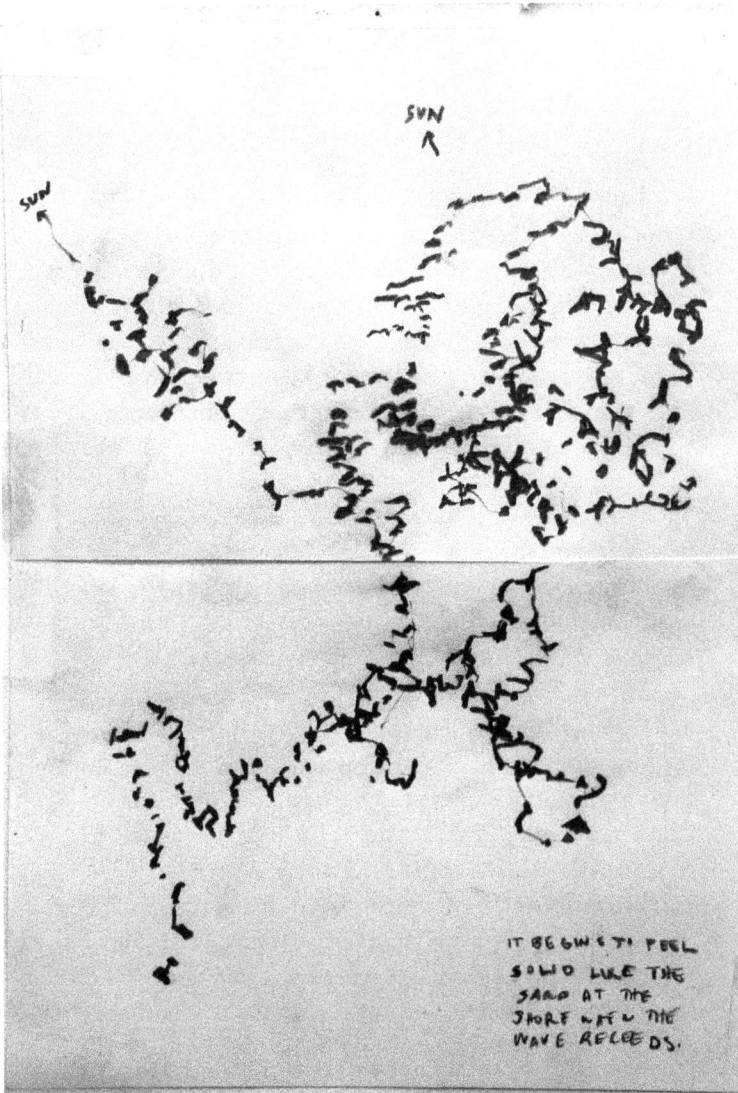

SUN

SUN

IT BEGINS TO FEEL
SOLID LIKE THE
SAND AT THE
SHORE WHEN THE
WAVE RECEEDS.

September 27, 2015
Full Lunar Eclipse
Corpus Christi, TX

Dear John,

I am drawing in the dark and the image of the moon is changing. It is changing at a rate that is similar to the speed of my drawing. If it were changing faster, I would loose my place while drawing. If it were changing slower, I would not be able to notice the change. The change seems similar to the rate of breathing and walking. It is only difficult to draw because I cannot clearly see my pencil and paper.

The darkness is also nice, because I let go of any worry about the drawing. It's a Full Lunar Eclipse.

How do we observe darkness? I am not curious about what darkness looks like when it is illuminated by lights. I am curious about observing darkness in the dark, especially when the darkness becomes velvety and the space becomes un-measurable.

How do we observe clouds, fog, smoke, the dark night and disorienting moments of light? How do we observe moving water? I will never forget what you told me, "You must look at moving water in a stream, not the water of a lake or an ocean, but of a stream, a stream that allows you to see its layers." The necessity is still present.

I recently had the fortune to draw from Turner's "Snow Storm- Steam Boat off a Harbour's Mouth." It has only one recognizable and measurable reference point: a vertical line that indicates the mast of a boat. I realized that without the mast, looking at the painting made me feel dizzy, as if

I were also getting tossed about in the waves. I think that measuring is one way in which we keep own bodies distinct, finite, outlined, materialized and localized in space. If we don't measure, do we, ourselves, disperse into infinite times and spaces?

With Love,
Amber

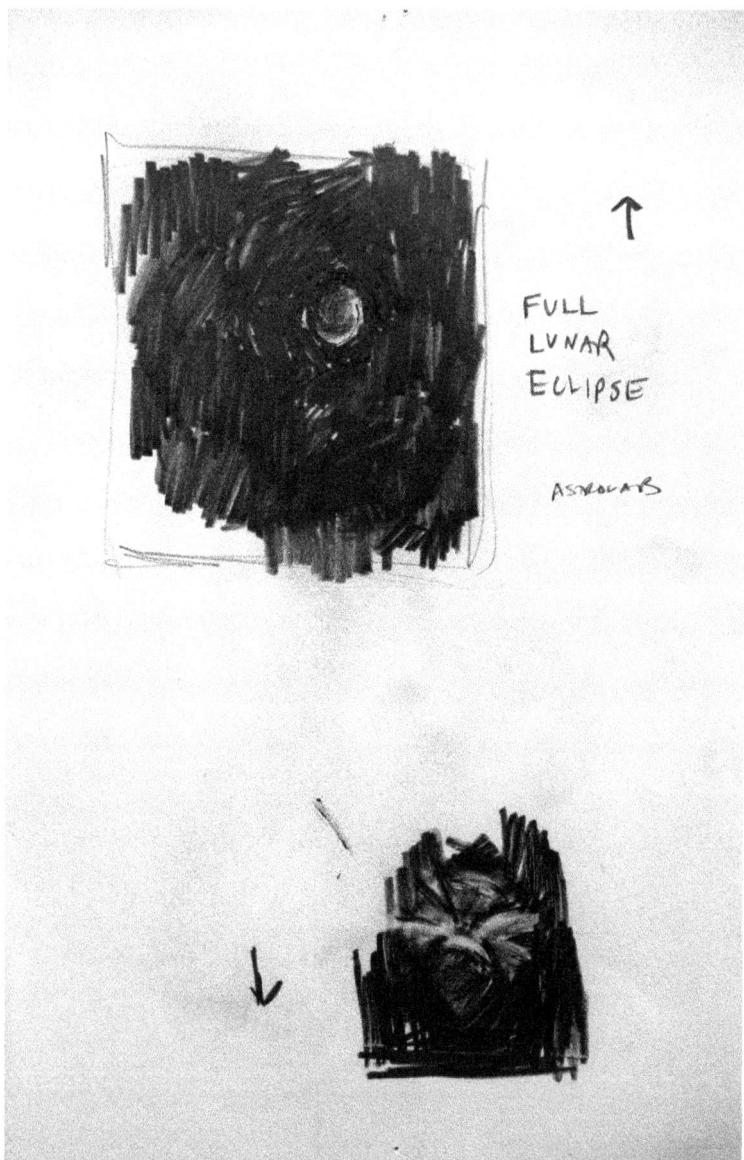

↑

FULL
LUNAR
ECLIPSE

ASTROLABS

Sigrid Hackenberg
y Almansa

Magic

I.

What is the desire for mysticism and magic? Why do we
mourn the loss of metaphysics and abstract expressionism?
Why are we fascinated with the idea of shamans?

Our common conception about the history of art tells
us that art began with magic. We have been taught to believe that cave art, in particular, served a magical purpose.

II.

Sigrid Hackenberg y Almansa is an artist and philosopher.
In discussing her work with my students, she recounted a
story about wanting to be a witch as a young child.

I see, now, a very small Sigrid. She is a tiny figure with
dark hair and determined, delighted, calm, fearless eyes.
She is looking out of a city window, imagining herself, flying. Pressed into her hand, she holds a small bottle. Inside
is a secret spell. It is secret because only Sigrid knows the
list of ingredients. Further, it is secret because one of the
ingredients can only be retrieved from a bird. You must be
able to recognize the bird and speak its language in order
to ask for the ingredient. Even then, the bird can say "no"
or "not today." The bird happens to love Sigrid and almost
always brings her the secret ingredient.

The spell allows Sigrid to step out of the window
gently, one foot at a time. She stands for a moment, on air.

She takes a deep breath. The air smells of rain and also of the bakery that is starting to turn out chocolate croissants. The sun hasn't begun to rise. The breath reaches all the way to her toes and tickles her. She giggles. She turns her forehead downward as if she were ducking her head under the water. She begins to swim. The air is cool but the water feels warm. She flies with the motion of the breaststroke, with several strokes taken without lifting her head. She flies through the night, over a city that is just as alive as an animal. She is exhilarated in the way that all children can be and most adults forget. She is humming to herself.

III.

As Sigrid grew older, her interest in magic became the substance of her art and her philosophy.

Children observe with no hardened knowledge of what is possible and what is not. Their world is naturally un-known and full of mystery.

I believe that magic is one name for the desire and the instinct to mimic the unknown. When a child finds discrepancies in her own knowledge, she doesn't ignore her knowledge or throw it out. She creates something.

Walter Benjamin writes,

"There is an old nursery rhyme that tells of *Muhme Rehlen*. Because the word Muhm meant nothing to me, this creature became for me a spirit: the mum-merehlen. The misunderstanding disarranged the world for me. But in a good way: it lit up paths to the world's interior. The cue could come from any-where. Thus, on occasion, chance willed that Kup-ferstichen (copperplate engravings) were discussed in my presence. The next day, I stuck my head out

from under a chair; that was a Kopf-verstich (a head
stick-out). If, in this way, I distorted both myself
and the word, I did only what I had to do to gain a
foothold in life. Early on, I learned to disguise myself
in words, which were really clouds."[38]

A child sees a bird flying. She has not yet seen a person
fly. She completes this inconsistency by imagining that
she can fly. The difference between the child and the adult
is that the child believes that it is possible to fly. She asks,
"How can I fly like a bird?"

IV.

As a child, I observed that time goes backwards and for-
wards, that the dead stay with us and that animals speak to
each other. If I wanted, I could also speak with animals. To
complete these tasks, I understood that I needed some kind
of magic: something that allowed me to make connections
where there were gaps in my knowledge. I can speak. They
can speak. What do I need in order to speak to them?

An adult who continues to mimic the unknown can
no longer say that she is conducting magic. The idea that
she is observing the unknown is, itself, already unacceptable; unbelievable except in extreme circumstances. The
unknown doesn't really exist. There is only the knowable
world, which has yet to be discovered.

As adults, we know that the magician does not really
make the women in the box disappear. We just enjoy the
question, "How does he do that?" This is not the sort of
magic that children employ. Children's joy resides in the
possibility that they too may be able to step into a box and
disappear. And they continue. Where does the disappeared

person go? Children imagine that another self will appear in another world. Or the person exists, but she has become invisible. Children easily accept the idea that there may be many selves, many worlds, invisible and visible realities and mysterious ways of getting to those places. Are they really wrong?

V.

To some, the unknown must be conquered, held, understood, calculated, named, exchanged and measured. To many adults, there is no need to conquer the unknown because it no longer arises in their consciousness. The sensory information that is gathered by the body is deleted before there's a chance to observe it. Our deleting processes are there to save energy. Why mull over information when there is no place to put it, no way to understand it and no way to use it? We are busy, after all.

Sigrid wakes us to the body's sensual desire to swim in the unknown. She reminds us that to think and read and imagine and observe and create is pleasurable, even erotic. Why wouldn't we feel caressed by an idea, aroused by a thought, intoxicated by a texture, excited by a form, overjoyed by a question?

There is an inconsistency between our common sense understanding of the world and our experience of being in the world. Let us not only acknowledge it, but also allow our selves to be inside of the body of joy, the unpredictable excitement of desire.

Why is the image of the philosopher a tired and serious old man, frowning and uncomfortable? Why can't the image of the philosopher be a magician-woman, shrieking with joy and flying through the night?

VI.

Why do we look nostalgically at magic, as if it were a home from which we have been exiled?

VIII.

We are taught that the earliest humans had no language, no currency and no religion. It is difficult for contemporary humans to imagine that world. When we try to transfer our contemporary functions for art to a pre-literate, pre-Christian, non-capitalistic society, we find no place to house art's meaning. In this absence, we say that art's function was *magical*. More specifically, we assume that early humans believed that their images were magical. As logical 21st century humans, we say that images are incapable of magic.

We work under an assumption that humans are evolving from less intelligent animals to more intelligent humans. Because of this linear understanding of our own history, we relate pre-history to our childhoods. We imagine that early humans must have been like us when we were very, very young. As children, we were able to believe in the impossible: to learn to fly, to speak with animals, to visit the dead or bring about thunderstorms with our minds.

Adults who remember this sensation and have lost it, mourn. Those who have forgotten the sensation, mourn nothing. But if they recognize it in others, they may feel spite and jealousy without understanding its source. This is because although they feel nothing, they recognize the space of the loss, which cannot be located or named. There is something out there that we are not connected to. And it stares at us. We feel it in the unbearable soft ache in the arches of our feet. We crave the sensation of being lost, of exploring a mysterious place and the freedom to do nothing, to think nothing. We fall towards this nothing-ness with the power of gravity. But we dutifully fight it. We dutifully stay on task.

VII.

Nearly everything in our contemporary lives fights open space, nothingness, the impossible, the unknown and the infinite. Only in silence can we hear the color and heaviness of the moon. Do you see the illuminated blue of the sky just before night falls? It's a blue that can't be painted. Like a ghost, it won't show up in photographs. But we have to allow ourselves the experiences that we can't take with us. We long for the wholeness we felt as children, when we were truly connected to inconsistencies of the world: the beauty and the terror of the unknown.

VIII.

Art is an activity that has never fit into the logic of Religion, Capitalism, Modernism, the Scientific Method, Classical Newtonian Physics, Enlightenment Thinking or any other overarching narrative. But we still operate within these systems. The incongruity is what makes room for magic. Our instincts tell us that we need some other way of being and some other way of getting there.

Art is one of the few activities that we have left, which has, at least in its imagined memory, a genetic connection to magic. Artists and philosophers have long been warned of the dangers of being seduced by magic, mysticism and mimicry. But let's be clear. We really don't know what magic is. That's the point. Magic is the name that we use for something un-namable. It is the term that we use to describe something that doesn't belong entirely to the realm of the known.

I believe that the desire for magic exists because we want to connect. And that connection is deeply routed to childhood. It is the last time, and for some people the only time, that we felt a connection to the unknown without a deep and sickening sensation of fear.

IX

Women, too, often belong to the category of the unknown.

Not very long ago, women were still regarded as being "child-like." Even today, people in positions of power denigrate the intelligence of women, as if it were acceptable and normal. They believe that women, like children, are incapable of high levels of intellectual, rational and critical thought. They wrongly assume that women are easily persuaded, impressionable and weak-minded.

Because the connection between women and children is often used as a misguided weapon, it is tempting to disregard the relationship. However, there is an important affinity between women, children and magic. The *fear* of magic and the *nostalgia* for magic are intertwined with an exile from the realm of the unknown. And what could be more unknown and mysterious, than the possibility and the capacity for birth, the ultimate mimesis? What could be more unknown, from the point of view of adults, than the child's ability to imagine, to think without knowing, to suspend belief and experience complete joy?

Historically, children have been physically connected to their mothers, especially in their youngest years. And so, if children embody the capacity to embrace the unknown, than mothers would be nearest to that capacity, if only to witness it and protect it.

It is quite obvious, but sadly it must be stated, that women and men are equally capable of complex thought. It is less obvious, but equally important, that although children may lack an accumulation of knowledge, they are also equally capable of complex thought. In some cases, given children's lack of common sense, children may be more capable than adults in terms of their ability to create clear, thoughtful and boundless ideas. Children are not impressionable and weak-minded. On the contrary they are stubborn, wild and rebellious. Adults, made uncomfortable by their inability to share a child's magical vision, become inflexible and scold the child.

X

Let us try not to fear what we do not understand. And when we do fear, let us try not to react with the violence of disbelief: the unmistakable urge to belittle and humiliate so that the unknown becomes less bright, less attractive, less important and more known. Instead, let's simply state that there is still something mysterious out there. There are still things that are not understood and escape our attempts to explain, locate and measure: consciousness, sex, art, love, childhood, birth, death and the infinite.

Magic is the space between our known world and the worlds we observe. It is the space that allows for Sigrid, the small witch, to get ready to fly.

Margaret Grimes

Theory

I.

In a small hill town in central Italy, where the morning mist fills the valley and leaves distant hilltops peeking up like islands in an ocean, I had an incredibly disorienting conversation. I was meeting Margaret Grimes for the first time. It was the fall semester of my second year in graduate school. Margaret was speaking with me as if we were family. It was more than that. It was as if we had been speaking about art, without barriers of ego or age or location or culture or history, for our entire lives. And then I realized. I already knew Margaret. I just couldn't *remember* knowing her, speaking to her, spending time with her. I couldn't remember meeting her.

I can still feel the sensation of that realization. We know each other but I don't remember you. It was exactly like waking up from a dream and finding yourself already awake: moving, dressed, working, driving, making art, having a conversation, teaching, laughing. But this conversation had been going on for several years, and although it was me, there, talking to Margaret, I do not remember any of it.

During the years that came directly before and after September 11th, I remember very little. I have some knowledge of the time period but only in the way that you begin to remember things from your childhood, things that people have been telling you about for years.

Upon realizing that Margaret already knew me, and that I had no recollection of knowing her, I began to do something strange that became second nature. I imagined that I knew her. I imagined that we had spoken. I imagined getting to know her. I imagined what our relationship would be like.

And at that point, all of my memories were created. I allowed them to be real. I had to. It was too embarrassing to tell her, "I don't remember meeting you." It was also too sad. How many moments did I miss? How many years? How many conversations, hugs, meals and adventures?

II.

Margaret once told me that at a certain point in her life, she wanted to paint what nature looked like. And then, something changed. She wanted to paint what nature felt like. And I realized, yes, there *is* a difference. There is a difference between what the world looks like and what the world feels like. Why is that? Why doesn't the photograph of a tree, for example, feel like a tree? This difference is only felt through constant, intense, direct observation. Margaret paints directly from nature.

Margaret and I have a similar desire to look for some overarching theory. We want something to replace Shamanism, Christianity and Modernism. The theory that we search for is not an explanation, formula or category. It is not a way to criticize or evaluate art. It is not a method or way to make art. It is something else. What?

III.

The term, "theory" became popular in the art world in New York City in the 90's. The word, "theory" was disar-

ranged by the telephone game. It travelled from Paris, and
from Europe in general, to New York City. The idea of
thinking about art became a strategy and formula designed
to justify art's existence. And this strategy became a
marketing tool.

During the theory wars, the "painter's painters" were
enemies of the "theory" people, who became the sole
owners of "postmodernism". This was like most fights:
boring and unpleasant. My painting teacher said, "Either
be an artist or join the enemy camp." The arguments were
only important in that they illuminated very specific fears
and vulnerabilities.

IV.

Margaret and I both feel the need to exist in a place that
acknowledges that the tree looks like this, some times, and
feels like that, sometimes. The tree, regardless of our endless observation, remains mysterious. The more we look at
it, the more it looks at us. We try to create the tree, but the
tree creates us. We try to separate ourselves, but we can't!
Margaret understands, intuitively, that I had to write. I had
to write *as* an artist.

V.

There is a Hegelian notion that manifests itself in our common sense, in the art world and in art education. It tells
us that we only begin to think about art, write about art
and philosophize about art when the making of the artwork is "done." There are three important ideas inherent
in this thought.

The first: Humans are evolving from creatures that use images for communication and magic towards humans who no longer need images at all. Images, to the rational human, are no longer necessary. They are only useful as artifacts that might trigger an intellectual reflection of the past.

The second: Thinking and making are separate processes. We must not *think too much* about art because it will disrupt the process of *making* art. In this scenario, art is like a child who plays and sings and climbs with glee until you ask, "What are you doing?" Then she suddenly stares at her toes and says, "Nothing and anyways, never-mind." Thinking it seems, might scare away the art.

The third: Painting, by which we mean "image-making", is dead. We don't need it anymore because we are rational, intellectual human beings. We only use art, in non-art disciplines, as instruments for reflection.

In the 90's, these ideas amounted to the creation of two parties; the postmodern theory people and the studio people; the observers and the makers, those who were ruled by intellect and those who trusted intuition, those who thought about art and those who made art. All the while, artists lived in fear that art was in fact dead, that everything new was already created, and that their practice was useless.

Although artists are most likely unaware of Hegel's ideas, they are quite aware of the fear, "*Don't over think it!*" and the idea that "*Painting is Dead.*" This is the most dangerous kind of fear. It's the fear that we assume is an inherent manifestation of our own limitations. In fact, it was articulated by a philosopher, about two hundred years ago, who was not an artist and had, at best, a marginal interest in the arts.

VI.

I try to write without closing down the space. There is a point, in painting as well, where an artwork feels raw and open. It's so exciting. We live for those moments. These are generous moments that give us potential, curiosity, space and opportunity. And there is a point, where a painting feels closed, finished and dead. You hardly notice this kind of painting, even if the maker is proficient and the painting is interesting in terms of content, subject, color and so on. The painting just seems to disappear. How can we keep open-ness? That is the mystery.

VII.

Writing is to see, to open awareness, to wake up in a space that you do not know. Try to wait. Try to hold out. Don't name it right away. Is that a window or a mirror? Am I inside or outside? Do we know each other? Try to allow yourself not to answer. Allow yourself one extra moment to be lost.

VIII

In September of 2003, I was apartment sitting for an acquaintance in Napoli. I had taken a nap and I woke up in confusion. I was there alone, which I had planned. I was looking forward to a few days of the constant, soft noises of the Centro Storico, the comfort of the rhythm of the city: animated but also relaxed, as if everyone were late but no one was worried. The city surprised me in that it was constantly welcoming me. I love New York, but New York rarely loves me back. Napoli, on the other hand, loves me unconditionally.

Napoli was a warm chaos and a beauty that I've never seen anywhere else. It was, for me, a safe haven. It was a place of un-ending surprise and a particular, exhilarating freedom. There were beautiful colors, sounds, textures and shapes. Everything was random and potentially disastrous, but somehow harmonious: the sounds of *motorinos* revving and screeching to a halt, drivers screaming, children playing cops and robbers, people answering their phones by leaning, from the waist, out of their tiny balconies "Pronto? Pronto! Pronto? Antonio, sei tu?," the fish monger announcing his goods by singing, the clanking of pots in the kitchen, old women lowering down their blue buckets so that grandchildren on the street below could place tomatoes and maybe lemons, maybe cigarettes, old men sitting out on the street in broken wooden chairs, smoking. There were meandering stones, stacks and layers of every material, piles building upward and piles breaking downward, doors inside doors inside doors. Buildings were replaced, reworked and rebuilt. The bright colors of laundry, whitened by the blinding sun, formed incredible compositions made accidentally by laundry lines and sheets. There was an ethical sensibility that suited me.

When I woke up, it was completely dark. I tried to understand what time it was. I was disoriented. The apartment had become sticky and shapeless. The room was not spinning, but it was breathing, growing and retracting. I wasn't alarmed, but I wanted to know. What was it that was so strange about the darkness? I walked to the window, four stories up, and looked down to the narrow street below. I heard fireworks. No, gun shots. Now plates being thrown, crashing in the street. Is it New Year's? No, of course not. It's September. A festival? A riot?

Slowly, very slowly, I realized the most obvious thing. There were no lights. The darkness extended all the way down the street. There must have been no moon. I had never once seen the city in the dark. Imagine how lovely it would be to explore our favorite cities, safely, at leisure, in natural darkness: a playground full of secret nooks and caves, open spaces to play red-rover, ladders to climb up and look-out spots to discover.

The first time that I arrived to Napoli, my train pulled into the station around two in the morning. It was raining and Piazza Garibaldi was full of prostitutes and seedy looking men. Someone picked me up from the street and put me inside a bar. I was given a *café*. The men, although they seemed dangerous, kindly told me how to find the nearest *pensione*. I stood at the buzzer of an unmarked building and asked, "Do you have a room?" An old lady gave me a small and clean room with a sink. I did not sleep. I rested with my eyes closed. In the morning, I feared that the whole city would be as ugly as Piazza Garibaldi and as dangerous as the train station, with everyone staring at you and trying to decide if you have anything worth stealing. Piazza Garibaldi was under construction. I couldn't tell how large it was, if there was a sidewalk or if the whole thing was a parking lot full of busses and taxis moving randomly. I dodged cars and prostitutes and endless crates of contraband cigarettes, sunglasses and signs for sex shows.

In the morning, I made my way toward the historic center and I quickly found my peace. The ground floor apartments had their windows and door open, revealing one room with a bed that was the same room as the kitchen, a table covered in plastic and some old, ornate, dark wooden furniture. Only the bathroom wasn't seen. People brought their chairs out onto the street. Cars barely fit down the roads. Gangs of kids played in the piazzas. I don't remember seeing any police.

Napoli was awake, always awake, but not like New York. Napoli wasn't working late into the night or getting dressed up for a big night out. Napoli was awake because it was still hanging out after dinner. The city is singing, discussing, eating and meeting in the piazza. Napoli feels dense and lively, but never claustrophobic. Like an old farmhouse, there are endless mysterious doors and odors, attic spaces and forgotten basements. The walls between the home and the street are moist and malleable like the insides of a body.

That night in September, Napoli had become like the countryside, with no stars and no moon. But instead of making my way through trees and bushes and wondering about animals, I was making my way through a three dimensional puzzle, with pieces missing and pieces broken, pieces fixed and altered, holes everywhere and strange geometric shapes. I couldn't tell if they were violent or happy.

Is it a terrorist attack? Suddenly this came to me. Those are not fireworks. We're under attack. No, I'm wrong again. We've already been attacked. Those are the gunshots of looters. We've lost power? Yes. Are there signs of distress? Nothing. I began to notice other people, leaning out of their balconies, asking each other, "*Ma che succede?*" (But what's happened?) My eyes were adjusting.

At first, in the dark you see nothing. Then, with time, you see formless shapes. I saw balconies, then people. Only at that point did the muffled noises become clear words.

Anything can happen in the short space following a disaster. My information came only from people leaning out of their windows and wondering out loud. I didn't have a cell phone. I didn't have a TV. I didn't have the Internet.

I didn't leave the apartment. I remember falling back asleep in a kind of unpleasant confusion, falling into abstract dreams about shapes accompanied by numbers and an evil kind of math.

The next day I found out that it was a blackout. There was a system failure somewhere in Switzerland. Terrorism had been ruled out.

VIII

This is what writing is, for an artist: the process of creating a space in which you have the chance to wake up, lost, and watch the world as your eyes slowly adjust, as the world observes you.

IX

The desire for an overarching theory is at least in part, a desire for more space: space to hold incongruity, irrational ideas, surprises and ruptures, horror and unspeakable panic, bliss, joy and the unnameable nothingness. We need a space that fights fear: the fear that if we observe ourselves making, we will scare the maker away, the fear of mimesis, the fear of failure and the fear that we are wrong in our observations that the world is both dead and alive, moving and watching us.

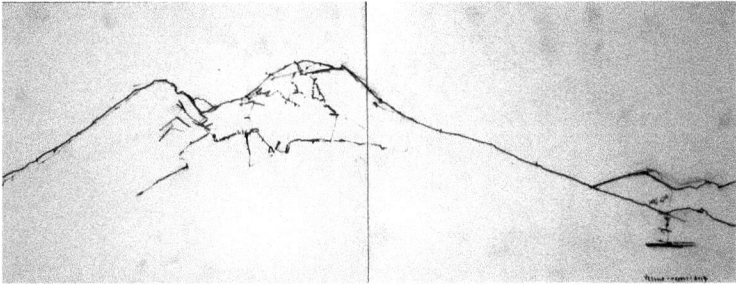

Louise Bourgeois
(1911-2010)

Checking

My friend once told me that Louise Bourgeois held studio visits called Sunday Salons in her home in Chelsea, New York. At this time, Louise was already quite famous and I could not believe that she would open her home to strangers. My friend gave me a phone number. I called. Louise answered. I asked if I could show her my artwork. She said, "Yes, come on Sunday." She gave me a time and an address and said goodbye. I was in shock.

I found the apartment. Someone opened the door that was not Louise and led me into a room where there were about a dozen other artists. The apartment was messy and full of books. There were several nervous people documenting the sessions with expensive equipment and foreign accents. There was a brightly dressed man who was either suffering from a mental illness or simply very eccentric. He was upset. There was a man with a sense of importance. There was whispering and a small commotion when it was understood that Louise did not want to come downstairs. She was upset about something, possibly relating to the brightly dressed man. We were given tea or maybe it was alcohol.

Louise came downstairs after about an hour of us all sitting in that small room. The artists became energetic and they were talking to each other as if they were attending a great party. I was sitting in a corner hoping that no one would talk to me. It was very warm. Louise came downstairs wearing a white outfit, that looked like cotton, which had many breasts hanging off from it. The breasts were also white and probably cotton. She was walking around in it as if it were completely normal. She was very small and full of energy. She was not angry, but also not calm. She was ordering people about. I was a little scared.

Recently, in the Capitoline Museum in Rome, I saw the "Statue of Artemis of Ephesus."[39] It is a Roman copy of a Greek statue, itself a copy of a pre-Hellenistic cult-statue, carved from wood, once worshiped in the Temple of Artemis. The goddess Artemis is a hunter and virgin, known for her protection of the wilderness, animals, women, childbirth, children. This particular version of Artemis has many egg or breast-like shapes hanging elegantly from her torso. Today, in my mind, Louise exists as Artemis.

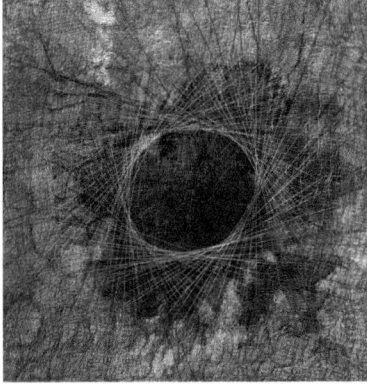

One by one, Louise looked at all the artists' artworks. I believe that people brought slides. She was critical, articulate, thorough, sharp, alive and bright. She was refreshingly ruthless. Her compassion was given through her honesty. I had the sense that she could instantly tell who was authentic and who was not. The term authentic is slippery, but that is the only way to put it. She was weeding out everything unnecessary, everything that was done for applause or for validation, everything weak in courage and honesty. Louise gave her criticisms in conversation with the important person. The rest of us were quite. I was the last one and I was hoping to be forgotten. Louise insisted that we look at my piece before everyone disbanded.

I brought my actual piece, not a slide. It is 18" by 18". It is made of carpenter's drop cloth stretched over a heavy wooden frame. The center is pulled back so that the fabric forms a bowl shape. A circle made from tangential lines is sewn into it. The circle floats on top of the cloth. It was made in Sevastopol, Ukraine in 2004 and 2005. I walked over to Louise and handed her the piece.

Louise said, "Bring me scissors!" Someone said, "No Louise. You cannot do that! Do not cut the strings! That is *not* your artwork." The order was made in a tone that you would use to scold a child, knowing that the child will not listen. It was a defeated command. I thought Louise might be offended. But Louise completely ignored the comments. She took the back side of the scissors and pressed against each one of the strings. She was careful. She checked them one by one. It took time. No one murmured. She wanted to see if they were all *taught*. She was checking. I smiled.

What does it mean to check?

Louise began to speak, but the man interrupted her. He was complementing me. But at this moment, I suddenly got courage. I said, "Please don't interrupt Louise!" He looked surprised. She made a small nod. And then she looked up. We made eye contact and she said, in a slow voice, like a child delighting in mischief, "Yes!"

Nicolas Carone
(1917-2010)

Newness

I.

I met Nick Carone as a young student in Italy when I was
19 years old. Nick called me the Madonna and asked,
"What kind of artwork do you make?"

I met Nick again as a graduate student when I was 22
years old, about a year after I had witnessed the attacks of
September 11 in New York City.

On the 10th, I had my first experience of panic. I had
an unbearable sensation of dread. I can barely think about
that day, which is, in some ways, much worse than the sensations of the 11th. On that Monday night, I stayed with a
friend who was living at Westbeth, an apartment complex
on the West Side Highway in downtown New York City.
I was told that some crazy artist lived upstairs. The next
morning, an endless stream of emergency vehicles poured
down the West Side Highway.

During my time in Italy, I visited Nick often. In his
space, feeling returned to me. Thoughts flooded my hands.
We shouted happily, disagreeing with each other about this
or that aspect of art. He told me the entire story of his life.
He told me about his childhood in Hoboken and his education as a young artist. He described drawing from Greek
and Roman statues. He told me about New York City in
the 1950's, the Stable Gallery Exhibition on 9th Street and
how he bought a house in Italy for a buck.

Nick talked often about metaphysics and about Matta. I had never heard the term before: *metaphysics.* As nick explained it, it was the activity of trying to see what is actually there. World, what do you look like? World, what do you taste like? World, what are you made of? This is drawing: an endless investigation into the being of the world.

There was no question of realism versus abstraction or postmodernism versus modernism, etc. It was not a process of categorizing or defining. It was the opposite. It was a question of allowing the world to be as it is: nameless, both dead *and* alive, both like this *and* like that. To Nick, drawing was not a practice or a skill or a way to begin a work of art. It was primal and sophisticated. Drawing was the embodiment of metaphysics. Drawing is to ask, with nothing other than the tools of your body, "What is being?"

Nick's eyes: lively and animated, serious but also laughing, determined, even when he was tired. His eyes have something in common with Napoli, that dirty and energetic city, which always seemed to be dancing at night or peacefully napping during the day.

Nick's home and studio: a space of energetic and boundless searching. His daily life, his rituals, his ideas, his philosophy, his history, his movements, his relationships to people and to Italy, the way that he casually kissed me and the tools he used to make art: they were all leaning on each other and creating each other. They were all necessary.

II.

I was intrigued by Nick's habit of going out into the countryside to hunt for rocks. When he found the right one, he would carry it back to his studio. There he carved a head

out of it. There were many of them, scattered about. I saw
some of his finished heads outside of his home, half hidden
by grass and flowers and weeds.

There were heads inside of the stones, waiting to be
discovered. Just as there were paintings inside of the caves.
Or rather there were creatures, which called out to humans, "I'm here!"

John Berger writes about visiting the rock paintings
in Chauvet, France. "The artist conversed with the rock
by the flickering light of his charcoal torch. A protruding
bulge allowed the bear's forepaw to swing outwards with its
awesome weight as it lolloped forward. A fissure followed
precisely the line of an ibex's back. The artist knew these
animals absolutely and intimately; his hands could visualize
them in the dark. What the rock told him was that the animals - like everything else which existed - were inside the
rock, and that he, with his red pigment on his finger, could
persuade them to come to the rock's surface, to brush
against it and stain it with their smells. [40]

Many years later, I visited Nick at his home in New
York City. I realized that the crazy artist living upstairs at
Westbeth, was Nick. Was he there on the 10th? Did he feel
it too? Can I re-imagine my life so that I was there with
him, instead? Instead of being alone? If I were there with
Nick, Nick who has been a soldier in World War II, Nick
who talked to me about art as if we were both teenagers,
equally desperate to find our way in this world, maybe
then, I would have not felt the panic.

When I think of Nick, I imagine him walking though
the Italian countryside, with his gorgeous, wrinkled, determined face, searching for his rock.

III.

Nick was one of the founding members of the New York
Studio School; the school that gave Modernists and Abstract Expressionists a place to call home as they fled the
destruction of Europe during the events of World War II.
The New York Studio School was made by the students
and for the students; a truly optimistic and democratic
experiment. It boasted the support of Hans Hoffman, William De Kooning, Meyer Schapiro, Mercedes Matter and
Philip Guston, amongst others.

In the 90s, New York City was filled with art- entre-
preneurs and fame seekers, cultural hoarders and hipsters.
My friend told me that the endeavor *to be known as an
artist*, is itself, the new art form. I found myself living
in the "end times". It was the end of painting, the end of
art, the end of meaning, the end of a century. Nick said,
"… the modern art movement as a revolution is over, it's
already known… It's a language that we are all still using
today and I think it's up to the individual to find his own
statement and his own mythology…"[41]

The language of the Modernists was a language of people who believed. In our mouths, the words became ironic,
disingenuous, metaphorical or derivative. I felt the weight
of apathy and of hopelessness, disguised by money, parties,
fame and opportunity. In the time of a borrowed language,
there is sorrow. We all need to feel that we have created
our own.

IV.

Nick told me about visiting the Venice Biennale in 1950
with Giorgio Morandi. Jackson Pollock's paintings were in
the American Pavillion. Nick wondered what Morandi, a

painter who spent all of his life painting a few small objects in the same small room, rarely venturing from his world, would think of Jackson Pollock. Nick said that Morandi saw the Pollock painting from a distance, from the corner of his eye. He immediately stopped and turned, fixed his sight on the painting and exclaimed with enthusiasm, "*Questo! Questo è nuovo!*" (This! This is new!)

V.

If we were *not* interested in newness, not because we crave sameness, but because everything is inherently already new, what would we think of Jackson Pollack? Another way to ask is this: If there were no word in our language for newness, how would Morandi have described the Jackson Pollack painting?

If newness were an abstract concept like God or the infinite, would it become more tantalizing? Or would it be casually set aside and forgotten? After all, no one attempts to create God. He is both already made and impossible to make.

VI.

Borges begins his short story, "The Immortal" by quoting Francis Bacon:

"Solomon saith: There is no new thing upon the earth.

So that as Plato had an imagination, that

Knowledge was but rememberence; so Solomon giveth

His sentence, that all novelty is but oblivion.

—Francis Bacon: Essay, LVIII"[42]

VIII.

Recently I read an article about the development of a two and a half year old. It cautioned the parents that at this age the child *still* believes that the parent can read his or her mind and visa versa. In addition, the child has trouble understanding the difference between you and me. It is assumed that the child is wrong.

After being taught, again and again, that he is wrong, that there is in fact a difference between you and me, that we are not connected, that we have barriers and boundaries, that we cannot hear each other's thoughts and feel each other's feelings, he begins to accept and believe. By the time that he is an adult, he has successfully turned off all sensations that convince him otherwise.

But what if we believed in something *else*? How would a change in our most basic beliefs about nature: about its separateness, its measurability, its ability to be new or old, how would a change in those beliefs affect how we observe, what we see, how we behave and what we make?

XI.

The experience of panic is often accompanied by a sensation of the self becoming separated from the body, of the self floating or falling.

Elena Ferrante writes about a Neapolitan woman named Lila who has just experienced the eruption of Mount Vesuvius.

> "Gasping for breath, she cried out that the car's boundaries were dissolving, the boundaries of Marcello, too, at the wheel were dissolving, the things and the person were gushing out of themselves,

mixing liquid metal and flesh… She used that term: *dissolving boundaries*. She said that the outlines of things and people were delicate, that they broke like cotton thread. She whispered that for her it had always been that way, an object lost its edges and poured into another, into a solution of heterogeneous materials, a merging and mixing. She exclaimed that she had always had to struggle to believe that life had firm boundaries, for she had known since she was a child that it was not like that- *it was absolutely not like that-* …She muttered that she mustn't ever be distracted; if she became distracted real things, which with their violent, painful contortions, terrified, her, would gain the upper hand over the unreal ones, which with their physical and moral solidity, pacified her; she would be plunged into a sticky, jumbled reality and would never again be able to give sensations clear outlines…A tactile emotion would melt into a visual one, a visual one would melt into an olfactory one, ah, what is the real world, Lenu, nothing, nothing, nothing about which one can say conclusively: its like that. And so if she didn't stay alert, if she didn't pay attention to the boundaries, the waters would break through, a flood would rise, carrying everything off in clots of menstrual blood, in cavernous polyps, in bits of yellowish fiber…She perceived herself as a liquid and all of her efforts were, in the end, directed only at containing herself. When, in spite of her defensive manipulation of persons and things, the liquid prevailed, Lila lost Lila, chaos seemed the only truth, and she- so active, so courageous-erased herself and, terrified, became nothing."[43]

XII.

Inspired by Nick, I have created the following definitions:

Panic: The sensation that a dangerous world is no longer respecting its boundaries; The sensation that everyone believes that boundaries exist when clearly they do not exist; A total untethering from the world, from objects and from one's own body; A continuously worsening sensation of isolation; A room too small is becoming ever smaller; A plane is endlessly circling the Earth and each time moving farther from the surface; The sudden sensation that you do not exist and you are watching the world like a ghost who watches a random movie.

Metaphysics: An attempt to answer the question, "What is There?"; An attempt to see what is there, rather than what we believe is there; An attempt to locate the observer in relation to the world; the activity of drawing.

Drawing: A way to enter into a present and physical relationship with the world; A form of research which involves no tool other than the body; A reciprocal process of observation.

Mimesis: The fundamental activity of all humans; A generative activity in which humans create their world by observing it.

Rock: The Skin of the Earth; A Boundary.

Paul Lindale

The Work of Art in the Age of the Anthropocene.

I. Karachay

Paul Lindale creates computer programs that draw. The drawings, which are viewed as projections, grow and change, as if an invisible hand were drawing as you watch. The drawings don't speak of computers or numbers or algorithms. Instead they references great landscape painters like Turner and Monet. Sometimes we see cities unfold and sometimes we see baron land or wind or water. But always, humans are absent.

Lindale's drawing program, *Karachay,* was projected in my small classroom in South Texas in 2014. The drawing program uses a random number generator so that each time it runs, it creates a new drawing. In theory, no drawing is ever the same. The drawings are like our experience of the world: It is in constant movement and perpetually escaping our desire to hold it tight.

The marks of *Karachay* resemble charcoal; velvety and smudged, erased and touched. As the drawing emerged before us, my students and I drew from direct observation. It took two hours. When we finished, we discussed our experience. Without any knowledge of the history of the place called *Karachay*, the students felt a sensation of loss and doom. Also, they said, it was beautiful.

Karachay is a lake in the former Soviet Union. In the 1950's, the Soviet Union started using Karachay as a dumping ground for toxic, radioactive waste, which was generated by a secret nuclear weapons factory. Karachay, and the area around it, is now considered one of the most

polluted places on Earth. In 1990, an international environmental advocacy group concluded that the radioactive levels
at Karachay could be deadly within one hour of exposure.

II. South Texas

My students in South Texas often spoke about the fact that
they found themselves attracted to places and objects that
were broken, forgotten and falling apart; the disgusting,
rotten and diseased. My student, Jen Olvera, told me that
given a chance to admire her mother's flower garden, she
found herself, instead, staring at a pile of broken TV's,
discarded in the neighbor's yard. My students felt a kinship
for ugliness.

What can explain this? Their cities are failing. The
water is un-drinkable. Drug-related violence is everywhere.
City centers are abandoned. Trash is endless. Healthcare
for women is intolerable, criminal. Manhunts, car thefts
and shootings are the usual. Humans are smuggled as if
they were fruit. I felt a particular tenderness towards these
students. They understood their situation to be normal.

There is something else that happened in South Texas.
A constant stream of students came to me to express sui-
cidal thoughts. They came from different circumstances,
but each repeated the same sentiment: "It must be, in some
way, my own fault."

III. The Anthropocene

"The Anthropocene" is a term used to describe a new
epoch in Earth's geological history; an epoch that reflects
the profound impact that humans have on Earth's environment. Paul Lindale is a particularly sensitive observer of

the Anthropocene. He creates artworks that expose people's relationship to the environment, and in particular, people's tendency to destroy.

In the age of the Anthropocene, the work of art seems destined to document the agonizing death of our world. Artists collect artifacts for a museum dedicated to the story of their own extinction. Images of destruction are constant: terror attacks, environmental disasters, wars, refugees and mass migration. Humans are moving, not by choice, but by necessity. They move in order to save their lives and the lives of their children.

What does it mean to be an artist in an age when humans appear to be not only manipulating our own environment, but destroying it? Are we the violin players who play as the Titanic sinks? Are we conflict journalists who report from the war zone? Are we scientists, trying to understand, through observation, the current state of affairs? Are we shamans, predicting the end through unknown powers? Are we the paparazzi, profiting from the public's consistent desire for images of disaster? Are we designers, on the wrong side of the affair, designing more efficient and beautiful ways to destroy the Earth?

VI. Mimesis
After the second plane hit the World Trade Center, my teacher looked downtown, toward the smoke. Then, he turned to me and said, "Isn't it beautiful?"

I said nothing and walked away.

Are artists, as Plato warned us, dangerous mimesis machines, copying without regard to content?

There is something that comes before our understanding of what is beautiful or what is true or what is good. Before all of that, we enact mimesis. We do it constantly: consciously and unconsciously. We do it at the cellular level and at the intellectual level. We do it as babies, learning to become ourselves. We do it as adults as we move through our everyday lives. We do it on social media.

Mimesis is the Greek term for copying. I use this term in order to call attention to the history of the concept. It is Plato who gave us our understanding of copying and we have not yet strayed from his perceptions. Plato told us not to mistake the shadow for the object. One is the original and one is the duplicate. The original exists. It is singular, unique and first.

Today, mimesis is not happening in a world of static, measurable, separate, original events. It is happening in a quantum world; a world of endless possibilities and uncertainties. Mimesis cannot be thought of as a rote process in which we simply duplicate what is there because what is *there* is entirely in question. "Quantum Art" suggests that we see, not what is there, but what we believe is there. When we observe, we make a choice and this choice creates our reality. The process is reciprocal. I create my reality and my reality creates me. Observation is therefore not a benign activity.

VII. A Child

A child is born and looks for love. She accepts whatever attention is given to her as such, as love, regardless of its substance. It is of the highest importance then, to ensure that the energies surrounding the child are positive.

An artist is born and begins to mimic. She accepts

whatever is around her as the material for mimesis, regardless of its substance. When she mimics her space or the objects within that space, she creates her world as such.

This is the fundamental difference between Plato's Mimesis and the mimesis of Quantum Art. When we copy something, we must be aware that we are not separate or quietly removed. We are not bystanders or documentarians or even critics or political activists. We are, by way of observation, quite literally, also creating the world that we live in.

And so, we must ask, what world surrounds contemporary artists today? And what world are contemporary artists creating as they enact the process of mimesis?

VIII. Violence

A child who witnesses a fight or an act of destruction invariably thinks that the event is his own fault. Of course he is not to blame. But look beneath the blame. There, in the child's brain, is the idea that he is capable of such an enormous task as creating the end of a relationship or a catastrophic environmental disaster. He believes that he is already powerful, in and of himself. He believes that he has this power without any particular tools or knowledge or relationships. Here is a moment to be optimistic. Here is the moment of the homogenerator!

IX. Homo Generator

Wolfgang Schirmacher created the term "*homo generator*" to describe contemporary humans; a species that has the ability to create life itself. Schirmacher writes, "Homo generator does not have to settle for what's given; he or she works instead, without any restrictions, with the fundamental building of life in all forms."

The child is, in some ways, correct. She does have the ability to create her world as she wishes. And if the world around her does not correspond with her desires, she feels pain. She feels responsibility. Instead of telling this child that she is wrong, we should encourage her to build her own world in accordance with her desires.

We are not simply witnessing the Anthropocene. We are also remembering it, imagining it and creating it. We have more choices than we acknowledge. We have, as children tell us, the ability to destroy the universe. But, simultaneously, we have the ability to create infinite new universes and new ways of behaving within those universes. We are not beholden to what we are given.

Jean Baudrillard reminds us, "Belief in reality is one of the elementary forms of religious life. It is a weakness of the understanding, a weakness of common sense, and also the final stand of the moral zealots, the apostles of the legality of reality and rationality who say that the reality principle can never be cast in doubt.[44]

And also, "Why couldn't there be just as many real worlds as imaginary ones? Why would there only be one real world? Why such an exception? In truth, the real world, among all other possible worlds, is unimaginable. Unthinkable, except as a dangerous superstition. We have to separate ourselves from it like critical thought once detached itself (in the name of reality) from religious superstition. Thinkers, try again![45]

Artists, here we are, observing the Anthropocene in the age of quantum physics.

Your ability to observe and the images that you create are also creating your world. You must ask yourself, "What kind of world do I desire?" Pay no attention to the limits of your so-called reality. They are made up.

Endnotes

1   Santiago Zabala, "Being is Conversation. Remains, Weak Thought, and Hermeneutics," published in "Consequences of Hermeneutics", pp. 161-176, Edited by Jeff Malpas and S. Zabala, Northwestern University Press, Evanston, IL, 2010

2   John Berger, "here is where we meet", p. 42, Vintage, New York and London, 2006

3   Santiago Zabala made this comment, while we were conversing via Skype in 2013. Zabala was speaking about his upcoming book, *Only Art Can Save Us Now*.

4   John Berger, "Drawing on Paper", p. 559, "Selected Essays", edited by Geoff Dyer, Random House, New York, 2001

5   Terrorist attacks at Charlie Hebdo in Paris, 2015.

6   Thomas Hugh, "The Spanish Civil War", Eyre and Spottiswoode, London, 1961

7   Marshal McLuhan, "Understanding Media: The Extensions of Man", MIT Press, Cambridge, 1964, re-print edition, 1994

8   Santiago Zabala, "Out of Network: The Art of Filippo Minelli" http://opinionator.blogs.nytimes.com/2013/04/16/out-of-network-the-art-of-filippo-minelli/

9   Ibid

10   William Kentridge, "Six Drawing Lessons", p. 11, The Charles Eliot Norton Lectures, Harvard University Press, Cambridge and London, 2012

11   http://www.egs.edu/faculty/alain-badiou/quotes/

12   Santiago Zabala writes, "Evidence that Heidegger at one time was a member of the Nazi party has led to a chilling effect on the way he is being studied, and remembered: his thought is once again being set aside because of his political adventure, and apparently racist views." https://lareviewofbooks.org/essay/what-to-make-of-heidegger-in-2015

13   Alain Badiou, "On Evil: An Interview with Alain Badiou." *Cabinet.* Issue 5, Winter 2001/2002

14   The Anthropocene refers to Earth's current geological time period. It is defined by the influence on Earth's environment

by humans.

15   Alain Badiou, "Is the word 'Communism' forever doomed?" *Miguel Abreu Gallery,* 2009

16   This idea has been paraphrased from my notes, which were taken during Alain Badiou's class in August of 2010 at The European Graduate School in Saas--Fee, Switzerland.

17   Jorge Luis Borges, "The Aleph and Other Stories", p. 160, Penguin Classics, New York, 2004

18   John Berger, "And our Faces, My Heart, Brief as Photos", p. 18, Vintage, New York, 1992

19   John Berger, "Selected Essays", page 8, edited by Geoff Dyer, Random House, New York, 2001

20   Walter Benjamin, "The Work of Art In The Age of Its Technological Reproducibility and Other Writings on Media", p, 25, Belknap Press, First Edition, Cambridge, 2008

21   Ibid, p. 24

22   Ibid, p. 24

23   Plato, "The Republic", Penguin Books, London, 1955

24   https://www.washingtonpost.com/world/italy-confirms-higher-cancer-death-rates-from-dumping-of-toxic-waste/2016/01/02/ecd9b838-b187-11e5-9ab0-884d1cc4b33e_story.html

25   http://www.filippominelli.com/cashemotherapy_update

26   John Berger, "here is where we meet", Vintage, New York and London, 2006

27   Sylvere Lotringer and Paul Virilio, "The Accident of Art", trans. Mike Taormina, Semiotext(e), New York, 2005

28   http://mahindrahumanities.fas.harvard.edu/content/william-kentridge-drawing-lesson-one-praise-shadows

29   Susan Sontag, "Regarding the Pain of Others", p. 125-126, Picador, London, 2004

30   Alan Lightman, The Accidental Universe, p. 27-28. Pantheon Books, New York, 2013

31   "Then Jesus said unto them, Verily, verily, I say unto you, Except ye eat the flesh of the Son of man, and drink his blood, ye have no life in you. Whoso eateth my flesh, and drinketh my blood, hath eternal life; and I will raise him up at the last day. For my flesh is meat indeed, and my blood is drink indeed." The Bible, (John 6:53-55)

32   Werner Heisenberg

33   Marina Abromovic, Performance: The Artist is Present, MOMA, 2010

34   David Brett, "What Is It, To think? What Is It, to Draw?", an essay published in "Entries. Drawings. 1999-2005" by Marisa Camino and John Berger.

35   Alain Badiou, "The Age of Poets", p 75, Verso, New York, 2014

36   Ibid, p. 77

37   Paul Virilio, "Art and Fear", trans, Julie Rose, Continuum Press, London and New York, 2003 and "The Accident of Art", trans. Michael Taormina, Semiotext(e), New York, 2005

38   Walter Benjamin, "Walter Benjamin's Archive", p. 109, editors Marx, G. Schwarz, M. Schwarz, Wizisla, Verso, New York, 2007

39   http://en.museicapitolini.org/collezioni/percorsi_per_sale/appartamento_dei_conservatori/sala_delle_aquile/statua_di_artemide_efesina

40   John Berger, "here is where we meet", p. 135, Vintage, New York and London, 2006

41   https://www.youtube.com/watch?v=J-kMxtJ0GfA

42   Jorge Luis Borges, The Aleph and Other Stories, p. 3, Penguin Classics, New York, 2004

43   Elena Ferrante, "The Story of the Lost Child", P. 175-179, trans. Ann Goldstein, Europa Editions, New York, 2015

44   Jean Baudrillard, "The Conspiracy of Art", p. 177, MIT Press, Cambridge, 2005

45   Ibid, p. 166